Oster Toaster Oven
Cookbook for Beginners 800

The Complete Guide of Oster Toaster Oven Digital Convection Oven with Large 6-Slice Capacity recipe book to Toast, Bake, Broil and More

By Robin Olsen

Table of Contents

Book Description

The Oster Toaster oven is one of the versatile and exceptional kitchen appliances that perform numerous functions successfully. It is one of the latest technologies that introduce some brand new cooking features.

If you are looking for value for money then the Oster Toaster oven is the only appliance that performs functions, than any other toaster oven can't deliver well. The Oster Toaster oven can heat the food faster, has a large capacity, and it's easier to clean.

The interior and exterior look is outclassed and it looks great sitting on the countertop of your kitchen. With its convection fan, the baking becomes so much easy. The person experience hand free cooking experience with user-friendly digital controls.

In this cookbook, we are covering not only the basic introduction but also we have prepared 80 delicious and mouthwatering recipes, using an Oster Toaster oven.

In this cookbook we will discuss:
- Introduction
- Basics Introduction for
- Oster Toaster Oven
- Cleaning & Maintenance of the Oster Toaster Oven
- Tips for usage
- How Does It Work? And Various Functions
- Recipes
- Conclusion

After using the Oster Toaster oven, you will find value for your money. It is one of the top-rated and top reviewed appliances. This guide serves well all the food lovers who want to make delicious and healthy recipes. Now, without sacrificing the taste, you can enjoy any range of meal you want by preparing item s in an Oster Toaster oven. No doubt it is an efficient appliance that has an edge over other countertop ovens.

Introduction for Oster Toaster Oven Cookbook

In this era of convection oven availability, an Oster Toaster oven is a top-selling appliance that is well-reputed for its functions and designs. It is a great quality product with a tag of the price that is affordable. And this appliance perfectly fit for household cooking.

What Is It?

The Oster Toaster oven enables the users to perform the function of boiling, roasting, baking, conventional baking, and toasting. It has a large interior that can hold up to 12-inch pizza and a whole turkey effortlessly.
- Brand: Oster
- Color: Black
- Item Dimensions: LxWxH (16.3 x 19.7 x 11.3 inches)
- Material: Stainless Steel
- Item Weight: 20.3 Pounds

How Does It Work? And Various Functions

The 7 preset functions include
- Toast Function
- Bake Function
- Convection Bake Function
- Pizza function
- Defrost
- Warm
- Broil

The Oster Toaster oven is a 6 slice convection toaster oven that has a large digital countertop and can fit a pan up to 2-inch height, 10.5-inch width, and 12.5-inch length.
Its temperature range is 150 to 450. The interior is light with 7 cooking settings. The oven comes with a baking pan, a crumb tray.
It runs on 1300 W.

No doubt an Oster Toaster oven is a good and attractive appliance, which fulfills your kitchen needs.

It is very good to perform toasting, baking, roasting, broiling, and crisping. It locks the nutrients of the meal and preserves the quality and texture. If you love toaster ovens then it would be a great addition to your kitchen, as it can cook bagels, bake cakes, and heat food like pizzas without making it soggy.

Multiple Heating Functions allow baking, broiling, toasting, and making breakfast, snacks, dinner, lunches without heating the kitchen and creating a bad odor.

Some of the other features of Oster Toaster oven:
- Easy design with one-touch LCD
- Plenty of accessories included in the package
- Easy to clean and maintain
- Larger capacity
- Convection mode ensures even heating
- Convenient digital display
- Breadcrumb tray is removable, hence easy to clean the toaster after cooking
- Timer constitutes 90 minutes

Things Need Attention

Burnt Smell from the First Use: Heat the oven for 15 minutes at 450 degrees F.
The oven is not turning on: Unit is unplugged Plug or less voltage is supplied, so you need to check both.
Meal get overcooked or burnt: It is because of incorrect temperate and cooking time, so the time and temperate needed to be set according to desire recipe needs.

Tips for Usage

If you are a beginner and using the oster convention Oster Toaster Oven for the first time then it is very important to follow some tips of usages.

- It is very important to remove the sticker after un-boxing the appliance.
- Open the door of the oven and remove any printed paper, stickers, and covering from the surface.
- It is very crucial to clean the racks, pans, and tray with hot warm water mixed with a small amount of dishwashing soap using a cleaning pad.
- Dry the unit completely before turning it on.
- Select a stable countertop location that is flat and airy.
- The plug should reach the socket easily.
- It is not recommended to modify the plug of the appliance.

- After turning the device for the first time if you smell smoke then do not worry as it is normal.
- The unit is designed for household cooking purposes only.
- The extension cord should only be used if proper monitoring and care are implemented, and also the electric rating should be equal to the appliance.

Cleaning & Maintenance of the Oster Toaster Oven

Cleaning the appliance
- The first step is to unplug the appliance and then allow it to cool if used for cooking.
- Clean the inner of the Oster Toaster oven with a damp cloth or towel.
- Don't submerge the oven into water.
- Use the mixture of mild soap and water and clean the unit brushes, baking tray, rack, and other accessories.
- Avoid cleaning it with chemical cleaners.
- Empty the tray of the toaster oven.
- The racks of the Oster Toaster oven are dishwasher safe.
- The outer surface of the oven can be cleaned with a damp cloth and then dry the oven with a dry cloth.

Safeguards and Maintenance

Whenever any electrician appliance is used it is very important to follow the basic safety measurements and precautions, as listed below:

- Do not touch the Oster Toaster oven when operating, and let the appliance cool before cleaning.
- Use the oven handles when moving the Oster Toaster oven.
- Do not immerse the appliance in water to protect the appliance from the electric shock.
- If the children are near the appliance then close supervision is needed to operate it
- The appliance should be kept away from the reach of children.
- The appliance should not be operated when the plug is damaged or the electric cord is broken.
- Use the manufacturer recommended attachments only.

- It is not recommended to place the Oster Toaster oven near a hot electric burner. The appliance may catch fire if the oster oven is covered or it touches flammable material like curtains and walls.

Do not place any material on top of the toaster oven.

It is necessary to keep an eye on all the parts as if any replacement or maintenance is needed.

Do not cover the oster oven with any metal foil, as it leads to overheating.

Cooking Timetable

Preheating time is not part of the cooking time table. Time varies with the weight and portion size of food. We recommend preheating the Oster Toaster oven before cooking meals in it.

Item	Time	Temperature
Steak (1-2 Pounds)	12 Minutes	400 Degrees F
Meatballs	10-12 Minutes	380-400 Degrees F
Fish	10-18 Minutes	380-400 Degrees F
Pork	12 Minutes	400 Degrees F
Whole Chicken	75 Minutes	360 Degrees F
Chicken Wings	10-15 Minutes	400 Degrees F
Lam , Chops, Meat	12-18 Minutes	400 Degrees F
Bacon	5 Minutes	400 Degrees F
Leafy And Green Vegetables	5 -10 Minutes	400 Degrees F
Potatoes	12-18 Minutes	400 Degrees F
Zucchini	12 Minutes	400 Degrees F
Pizza	5-10 Minutes	400 Degrees F
French Fries	`18 Minutes	400 Degrees F
Burger	10-15 Minutes	360-380 Degrees F

Chapter 1: 10 Brunches

Delicious Potato Pancakes

Preparation Time: 25 Minutes
Cooking Time: 20 Minutes
Yield: 4 Servings
Ingredients
4 Idaho potatoes, washed, peeled, and shredded
4 ounces onion, peeled and diced
1 egg, organic
1/3 teaspoon baking powder
2 tablespoons all-purpose flour
2 tablespoons vegetable oil, canola oil
Salt and freshly grounded black pepper, to taste

Mango Vinaigrette Ingredients
4 ounces mango nectar
1/3 teaspoon pickled jalapeno pepper, minced
2 ounces lemon juice
2 teaspoons mango, diced
2 ounces olive oil
Salt and black pepper, to taste

Directions
Turn on the Oster Toaster oven to convection bake function setting.
Whisk all the mango vinaigrette ingredients in a bowl and set it aside to be served later on.
The first step is to wash, peel, and whir the potatoes using a food processor.
Transfer the potatoes from the food processor to the mixing bowl.
Add egg, onions, baking powder, salt, and black pepper to the bowl.
 Add a small amount of flour and mix.
Bind all the ingredients well.
Heat oil in a skillet and place pancake on the surface of the skillet.
Cook until edges dry out, from both sides.
Turn on the Oster Toaster oven and set the temperature to 350 degrees F.

Now put the pancakes onto the baking rack of the toaster oven and cook pancakes in the Oster Toaster oven for few minutes by turn on the bake function.
Once crispy and golden, take out and serve with already prepared sauce.

Nutrition Facts
Servings: 4
Amount per serving
Calories   517
% Daily Value*
Total Fat 21.5g   28%
Saturated Fat 3.7g 19%
Cholesterol 41mg 14%
Sodium 41mg   2%
Total Carbohydrate 76g 28%
Dietary Fiber 5.9g 21%
Total Sugars 38.3g
Protein 5.8g

Biscuits in Oster Toaster Oven

Preparation Time: 25 Minutes
Cooking Time: 12 Minutes
Yield: 8 Servings
Ingredients
2.5 pounds all-purpose flour
1 tablespoon salt
1/4 cup baking powder, plus 1 tablespoon
1/2 pound lard
5-1/2 cups buttermilk
1 teaspoon melted butter, topping
Directions
Turn on the Oster Toaster oven to convection bake function setting.
Preheat the oster oven to450 degrees F.
Take a large mixing bowl and add lard.
Turn on the mixer and start adding buttermilk to the lard.
Now, add flour, little at a time.
Then add salt and baking powder.
Once dough is formed transfer it to a work area.
Roll the dough well and cut into a 1-inch thickness.
Prick dough using a fork.
Cut the biscuit with the cutter and then place it on a baking sheet that is lined with parchment paper.
Bake it in an oster oven for 12 minutes.
Afterward, brush the tops of biscuits with melted butter. Serve and enjoy.

Nutrition Facts
Servings: 8
Amount per serving
Calories   840
% Daily Value*
Total Fat 31.1g   40%
Saturated Fat 12.2g   61%
Cholesterol 33mg 11%
Sodium 1042mg   45%
Total Carbohydrate 119g   43%
Dietary Fiber 4g   14%
Total Sugars 7.7g
Protein

Cake with Berries

Preparation Time: 20Minutes
Cooking Time: 10 Minutes
Yield: 6 Servings
Ingredients
18 ounces almond flour
1 cup powdered sugar, sifted
3/4 cup all-purpose flour
6 egg whites
1-1/3 cups melted butter, plus some for molds
1/3 teaspoon almond extract

Berries Ingredients
2 cups strawberries, sliced
4 tablespoons sugar, granulated
Directions
Turn on the Oster Toaster oven to convection bake function setting.
Preheat the oster oven to 400 degrees F.
In a large bowl, mix egg whites using a hand beater until stiff peak on top.
Add in melted butter and almond extract.
Now in a bowl, shift dry ingredients and add them to the egg mixture.
Spread the prepared batter into molds
Bake it in the Oster Toaster oven for 10 minutes using the bake function, until golden around the edges. Meanwhile, mix berries with sugar.
Place the cake on a serving plate and serve with berries.

Nutrition Facts
Servings: 6
Amount per serving
Calories   949
% Daily Value*
Total Fat 73.1g   94%
Saturated Fat 22.5g   112%
Cholesterol 81mg 27%
Sodium 252mg   11%
Total Carbohydrate 61.8g   22%
Dietary Fiber 10.4g37%
Total Sugars 33.3g
Protein 23.9g

Filled Puff Pastry

Preparation Time: 25 Minutes
Cooking Time: 18 Minutes
Yield: 3-4 Servings
Ingredients
2 pastry sheets, defrosted

Savory Filling Ingredients
1/3 cup green olives
1/3 cup parsley leaves
1 clove garlic
2 tablespoons olive oil
½ cup spinach leaves

Sweet Filling Ingredients
1.5 cups whole fresh cranberries
3/4 cup dark brown sugar
1/3 cup pecans
2 teaspoons butter

Directions
Turn on the Oster Toaster oven to convection bake function setting.
Take a food processor and then finely chop the olives, parsley, garlic, olive oil, and spinach leaves, which will prepare the savory filling ingredients. (Do not make it a paste).
Now prepare the sweet filling, for that combines all the sweet filling ingredients in a food processor until finely chopped, don't make it a paste.
Unfold the pastry sheet and place it on to baking dishes.
Spread the sweet filling on top of the savory filling.
Now place it in the center of the pastry.
Crimp the edges of pastry dough, so that the lip around the edge forms.
Bake in Oster Toaster Oven at 400 Degrees F, for about 18 minutes, by clicking the bake button.
Once pastries are golden brown, take out and serve.

Nutrition Facts
Servings: 3
Amount per serving
Calories   575

% Daily Value*
Total Fat 33.4g   43%
Saturated Fat 5.1g 25%
Cholesterol 7mg   2%
Sodium 286mg   12%
Total Carbohydrate 68.8g   25%
Dietary Fiber 5.2g 19%
Total Sugars 42.6g
Protein 6.1g

Savory Bread Pudding with Asparagus and Dried Tomatoes

Preparation Time: 30 Minutes
Cooking Time: 55-60 Minutes
Yield:4 Servings
Ingredients
4 tablespoons olive oil
1 large green onion, sliced
2 cups of asparagus, cut into 1-inch length
½ cup fresh leeks, chopped
1 cup sliced mushrooms
1/2 cups grated Gruyère cheese/Swiss cheese
1 cups goat cheese, crumbled
1/3 cup dehydrated tomatoes
1/3 cup chopped parsley
3 tablespoons thyme leaves
4 large eggs
1/2 cup grated fontina
1 cup whipping cream
1-1/2 cup milk
4 cups bread, cut into small pieces
Salt and black pepper, to taste
Oil spray, for greasing

Directions
Turn on the Oster Toaster oven to convection bake function setting.
Set the temperature to 350 degrees F.
Take a square pan that is 8 inches and grease it with oil spray.
Take a skillet and sauté onions in oil.
Cook the onions and then add asparagus, mushrooms, and leeks.
Cook it for 4 minutes.
Set it aside for further use.
Now take a bowl and mix cheeses, dried tomato, and herbs.
Whisk eggs, whipped cream, milk, salt, and black pepper in a medium bowl.
Layer the half bread pieces in the baking pan and spread half of the
asparagus mixture and half cheese mixture on top.
Now pour the half egg mixture over cheese.
Repeat the steps with the remaining bread, cheese mixture, asparagus mixture,
and egg mixture.
Let it sit for a few minutes so that the ingredients are submerged into the bread.

Bake the pudding in the Oster Toaster oven for 40 minutes. Then serve.

Nutrition Facts

Servings: 4

Amount per serving

Calories 888

% Daily Value*

Total Fat 60.7g 78%

Saturated Fat 28.8g 144%

Cholesterol 315mg 105%

Sodium 837mg 36%

Total Carbohydrate 45.9g 17%

Dietary Fiber 8.5g 30%

Total Sugars 11.9g

Protein 45.6g

Cinnamon Toast

Preparation Time: 20 Minutes
Cooking Time: 12 Minutes
Yield: 1 Serving
Ingredients
1 tablespoon brown sugar
2 teaspoons margarine, room temperature
1/4 teaspoon cinnamon
Pinch of nutmeg
2 slices whole-wheat or multigrain bread

Directions
Mix brown sugar, cinnamon, nutmeg, margarine in a mixing bowl and whisk it with a fork.
Spread the mixture over the bread slices equally.
Toast the bread in the Oster Toaster oven, using toast function, until the sugar melted and the bread gets brown.
Serve hot.

Nutrition Facts
Servings: 1
Amount per serving
Calories   242
% Daily Value*
Total Fat 9.9g   13%
Saturated Fat 1.8g 9%
Cholesterol 0mg   0%
Sodium 310mg   13%
Total Carbohydrate 32.1g   12%
Dietary Fiber 4.2g 15%
Total Sugars 12.1g
Protein 7.1g

White Corn Cookies

Preparation Time: 20 Minutes
Cooking Time: 12 Minutes
Yield: 3 Servings
Ingredients
2/3 cup all-purpose flour
3/4 cup sugar
3/4 cup white cornmeal
8 tablespoons butter
3/4 cup honey
2 egg whites
Oil spray, for greasing

Directions
Turn on the Oster Toaster oven to convection bake function setting.
Preheat the Oster Toaster oven at 350 degrees F.
Take a bowl and combine cornmeal, sugar, and flour.
Add in butter and mix well.
Then add honey and egg whites, and continue beating until no lump remains.
Use a hand mixer to mix all the ingredients well.
Once the mixture is smooth, drop the cookie dough on to oil grease cookie sheet.
Bake it in the Oster Toaster oven until cookies get brown for about 12-15 minutes.

Nutrition Facts
Servings: 3
Amount per serving
Calories   792
% Daily Value*
Total Fat 31g   40%
Saturated Fat 19.5g   97%
Cholesterol 81mg 27%
Sodium 244mg   11%
Total Carbohydrate 124.2g   45%
Dietary Fiber 2.3g 8%
Total Sugars 70.9g
Protein 8.5g

Spiralized Potato Gratin

Preparation Time: 20 Minutes
Cooking Time: 70 Minutes
Yield: 4 Servings
Ingredients
2 tablespoons olive oil
4 shallots, minced
2 clove garlic, minced
1/3 cup white wine
1 cup heavy cream
1 cup vegetable broth
2 tablespoons sage
1 teaspoon Dijon mustard
Salt and pepper, to taste
2/3 cup grated Parmesan cheese, divided
1 cup shredded Cheddar cheese
1 1/2 pounds sweet potatoes, peeled
1 1/2 pounds Yukon Gold potatoes, peeled
1/3 cup fresh bread crumbs
2 tablespoons butter, melted
1 teaspoon parsley, fresh

Directions
Preheat the Oster Toaster oven at 375 degrees F.
Heat olive oil in a saucepan and cook shallots and ginger in it for one minute.
Then pour in the wine and then reduce it to half
Then add the cream, salt, pepper, mustard, and sage
Cook and then remove it from heat
Add half of the parmesan cheese and cheddar cheese.
Set it aside for further use.
Now spiralized the sweet potatoes and add them to a bowl.
Toss it with prepared sauce and put it on to a greased casserole dish.
Toss bread crumbs on top along with remaining cheese, butter, and parsley.
Cover casserole with foil.
Bake it in an Oster Toaster oven for 40 minutes.
Then uncover and bake it for 30 more minutes.
Remove it from the oven, serve, and enjoy.

Nutrition Facts

Servings: 4

Amount per serving

Calories 735

% Daily Value*

Total Fat 40.6g 52%

Saturated Fat 21.9g 109%

Cholesterol 106mg 35%

Sodium 782mg 34%

Total Carbohydrate 69.5g 25%

Dietary Fiber 8.8g 31%

Total Sugars 2.4g

Protein 23.3g

Eggs Benedict with Crab

Preparation Time: 25 Minutes
Cooking Time: 15 Minutes
Yield: 4 Servings
Ingredients
1/3 cup vegetable oil
½ cup parsley
2 teaspoons vinegar
6 cups water, or as needed
4 eggs
6 bacon slices, cooked
2 English muffins
6 crab claws, cooked

Hollandaise Sauce Ingredients
4 egg yolks
2 tablespoons unsalted butter, melted and hot
2 tablespoons hot water
2 tablespoons lemon juice
Salt and black pepper, to taste

Directions
Take a blender and pulse parsley and vegetable oil.
Pour it in to squeeze bottle.
In a skillet bring water and vinegar
 Let it boil.
Pour eggs into the water.
Let eggs cook for 5 minutes.
Remove eggs with a slotted spoon.
Drain it on a paper towel.
Put the English muffins in Oster Toaster oven and bake it until golden brown, for 10 minutes
Now prepare the sauce and for that take a blender and blend water, lemon, and egg yolks.
While the blender is running pour the butter into the blender.
Add seasoning of salt and pepper.
Now assemble the egg and for that top each muffin with bacon, poached egg, and crab claw.
Pour blender sauce on top.

Enjoy with the drizzle of parsley sauce.

Nutrition Facts

Servings: 4

Amount per serving

Calories   1205

% Daily Value*

Total Fat 84.8g   109%

Saturated Fat 25.9g   129%

Cholesterol 779mg   260%

Sodium 3656mg   159%

Total Carbohydrate 15.6g   6%

Dietary Fiber 1g   4%

Total Sugars 1.7g

Protein 93.3g

Blueberry Cakes

Preparation Time:25 Minutes
Cooking Time: 30 Minutes
Yield: 3 Servings
Ingredients
1-1/4 cups cake flour
1/4 teaspoon baking soda
1/4 teaspoon cream of tartar
1/4 teaspoon salt
2 eggs
3/4 cup sugar, plus some for pan
3/4 cup heavy cream
¼ pint of blueberries, fresh

Lemon Syrup
1 cup of sugar
1 cup of water
1 tablespoon lemon zest

Directions
First, prepare the lemon syrup.
Combine sugar with water in a saucepan and bring the water to a boil.
Then put the lemon zest and simmer the mixture for 10 minutes.
Remove it from heat.
Let it get cool and reserve for further use.
Now prepare the muffins.
Preheat the Oster Toaster oven at 350 degrees F.
Sift together the baking soda, cream of tartar, flour, and salt a few times.
Take about 1/4 cup and reserve it.
Take a bowl and whisk the egg and sugar with a hand beater.
In a separate bowl, whip the heavy cream until soft peak on top.
Add the cream into the egg mixture
In the end, mix it with dry ingredients as well as the reserved 1/4 cup of dry mix.
Gently fold in blueberries.
Do not over mix the blueberries in batter.
Oil grease a muffin tin and then lined buttered muffin cups.
Spoon the prepared batter into muffin cups.
Bake the cups in the Oster Toaster Oven for 15 minutes.
Once done, serve with lemon syrup.

Nutrition Facts

Servings: 3

Amount per serving

Calories 759

% Daily Value*

Total Fat 14.6g 19%

Saturated Fat 7.9g 39%

Cholesterol 150mg 50%

Sodium 373mg 16%

Total Carbohydrate 153.7g 56%

Dietary Fiber 2.1g 7%

Total Sugars 118.5g

Protein 9g

Chapter 2: Beef, Pork, & Lamb

Brie Bruschetta

Preparation Time: 20 Minutes
Cooking Time: 10-15 Minutes
Yield: 3 Servings
Ingredients
6 rounds country loaf, 1/3 inch thick
4 tablespoons balsamic vinegar
4 tablespoons olive oil
Salt and black pepper, to taste
6 ounces of brie
7 ounces of artichoke hearts, marinated and drained
½ tablespoon mint, chopped and fresh
2 Ounces of ham
1 tablespoon basil, chopped
1 medium red onion, chopped
1/3 cup parmesan, grated
1 tablespoon garlic, chopped

Directions
The first step is to set the Oster Toaster oven to broil and let it preheat for a while.
Take a baking pan and arrange the bread in a layer on the pan.
Drizzle few splashes of olive oil on top and then season it with salt and black pepper.
Transfer the baking pan to the oven rack.
Broil the bread until golden brown.
Afterward, take out the bread and layer it with brie.
Wash and cut the artichokes into thick slices.
 Heat remaining olive oil inside a heavy bottom skillet on low to medium heat.
Then put garlic and onions inside.
Stir it well and then add artichokes and ham.
Pour in the balsamic vinegar, salt, pepper, basil, and mint.
Spoon this mixture over the bread.
Sprinkle the Parmesan cheese on top. Serve and enjoy.

Nutrition Facts

Servings: 3
Amount per serving
Calories   835
% Daily Value*
Total Fat 45.1g   58%
Saturated Fat 18.4g   92%
Cholesterol 94mg 31%
Sodium 1635mg   71%
Total Carbohydrate 67.9g   25%
Dietary Fiber 6.8g 24%
Total Sugars 2.6g
Protein 39.7g

Herbed and Mustard Pork Tenderloin

Preparation Time: 20 Minutes
Cooking Time: 50 Minutes
Yield: 4 Servings
Ingredients
2 pounds of pork tenderloins
6 cloves garlic, peeled and minced
4 tablespoons Dijon Mustard
8 Potatoes cut in quarters
2 tablespoons rosemary, chopped
4 tablespoons olive oil
2 tablespoons fresh thyme, stemmed
Freshly grounded black pepper, to taste
Oil spray, for greasing
Salt, to taste
Directions
The first step is to preheat the Oster Toaster oven to 375 degrees F.
Take a large bowl and mix Dijon mustard, rosemary, thyme, salt, pepper, and garlic. Rub this mixture over the pork tenderloins.
Put the tenderloin on to baking tray that is greased with oil spray.
Make sure the baking sheet or tray fits inside the oven conformably.
Put the potatoes beside the pork tender ions. Drizzle the olive oil on top.
Now set the function to bake and adjust the timer to 30 minutes.
After the time completes, remove the baking tray and cover it with aluminum foil If necessary cook the potatoes for 20more minutes by placing it inside the oven rack. Then serve and enjoy.
Nutrition Facts
Servings: 4
Amount per serving
Calories   897
% Daily Value*
Total Fat 34g   44%
Saturated Fat 9g   45%
Cholesterol 213mg   71%
Sodium 389mg   17%
Total Carbohydrate 71.2g   26%
Dietary Fiber 12g   43%
Total Sugars 5.1g
Protein 76.1g

Stuffed Beef Tenderloin

Preparation Time: 20 Minutes
Cooking Time: 60 Minutes
Yield: 4 Servings
Ingredients

Main Ingredients
2 pounds of beef tenderloin
1-1/4 cup beef broth
2 tablespoons of unsalted butter
Vegetable oil, as needed

Ingredients for The Filling
4 ounces fried bacon, chopped
4 ounces chicken breast
1/3 cup cream
1/3 tablespoon rosemary, chopped
½ tablespoon thyme, chopped
1 tablespoon sage, chopped
½ tablespoon Chinese onion or chives, chopped
2 tablespoons parsley, chopped
Salt and black pepper, to taste

Ingredients For The Sauce
1/3 cup dry red wine
2 shallot, chopped
 1 carrot, chopped
2 garlic clove
1/3 cup beef broth
4 ounces butter
2 tablespoons of olive oil
Salt and black pepper, to taste

Directions
Mix all the sauce ingredients in a bowl, and set aside for further use.
The first step is to clear the beef tenderloin.
Take a blender and pulse together chicken, rosemary, thyme, sage, onions, parsley, bacon, salt, black pepper, cream.
Rub the beef with the rub, and spread the stuffing.

Roll the beef tenderloin with kitchen twine.

Take a skillet and brown beef in it by heating oil and butter

Once the tenderloin sear adds in the beef broth.

Then add sauce and cover the skillet.

Let it cook for40 minutes, and transfer the tenderloin from the cooking skillet to the baking tray.

Turn on the Oster Toaster oven and set it to 400 degrees F.

Put the baking tray inside the oven and let it cook for 20 minutes.

Meanwhile, reduce skillet sauce to half and serve over cooked tenderloins.

Enjoy hot.

Nutrition Facts

Servings: 4

Amount per serving

Calories   1050

% Daily Value*

Total Fat 74.1g   95%

Saturated Fat 32.6g   163%

Cholesterol 338mg   113%

Sodium 1123mg   49%

Total Carbohydrate 4.7g 2%

Dietary Fiber 0.9g 3%

Total Sugars 1.6g

Protein 84.5g

Meatloaf

Preparation Time: 20 Minutes
Cooking Time: 50-60 Minutes
Yield: 2-3Servings
Ingredients

1/3 cup milk
6 slices white sandwich bread, torn
1 pound beef, ground
1 pound pork, ground
4 small onions, finely chopped
4 cloves garlic, minced
1/2 cup chili sauce
1/4 cup ketchup
1 cup parsley, chopped fresh
1/2 cup Parmesan cheese, grated
4 eggs, lightly beaten
Salt and freshly ground pepper
2 tablespoons brown sugar

Directions
Preheat the Oster Toaster oven to 350 degrees F.
Put the rack at the bottom.
Take a large bowl and pour the milk and bread on top
Let the bread soak up the milk.
Then add pork, beef, garlic, onion, half chili sauce, eggs, salt, pepper, half ketchup, half parmesan cheese, and parsley.
Divide this mixture in half and make two meatloaf logs.
Bake it in the Oster Toaster oven for 50 minutes.
 Now combine half of the chili sauce and half of ketchup and brown sugar in a small bowl and prepare the glaze.
Brush this prepares glaze on top of loaves and bake it in the Oster Toaster oven until juices run clear.
The internal tempura should be 160 degrees F at the end of cooking.
Remove meatloaves from the oven and let it rest for 5 minutes.
Once done, serve and enjoy

Nutrition Facts

Servings: 3
Amount per serving
Calories   1041
% Daily Value*
Total Fat 32.6g   42%
Saturated Fat 12.6g   63%
Cholesterol 486mg   162%
Sodium 2256mg   98%
Total Carbohydrate 71.7g   26%
Dietary Fiber 3.9g 14%
Total Sugars 22.7g
Protein 113.1g

Venison With Veggies

Preparation Time: 20 Minutes
Cooking Time: 40 Minutes
Yield: 4 Servings
Ingredients

Venison Ingredients
4 venison loin steaks, 6-ounce each
4-1/2 teaspoons coriander seeds, cracked
5 allspice powder
1 cinnamon powder
2 cups Pinot Noir wine
1 cup beef glaze
1 tablespoon of Butter
Salt and black pepper, to taste

Vegetable Ingredients
1 cup Fava beans
25 asparagus spears

Directions
Preheat the Oster Toaster oven to 400 degrees F.
The first step is to roll the venison in salt, pepper, and coriander seeds.
Next, take a skillet and cook add all-spice, cinnamon, and wine, and reduces it to 90 % half.
Now the glaze is prepared, and then adds in butter to it.
Add glaze and reduce by half.
Now, cook the steak by placing it on a baking sheet inside the Oster Toaster oven and cook until the internal temperate reaches 160 degrees F.
Meanwhile, blanch the vegetables in hot water for 1 minute and then put them in an ice-water bath
Once 2 minutes remaining for the steak to be cooked add vegetable and turn on the broil of the Oster Toaster oven.
Cook for 2 minutes, and then serve the steak with vegetables.

Nutrition Facts
Servings: 4
Amount per serving
Calories   1831

% Daily Value*

Total Fat 51.9g 67%

Saturated Fat 33.6g 168%

Cholesterol 207mg 69%

Sodium 11966mg 520%

Total Carbohydrate 309.7g 113%

Dietary Fiber 12.6g 45%

Total Sugars 99g

Protein 60.6g

Roast Beef

Preparation Time: 30 Minutes
Cooking Time: 15-40 Minutes
Yield: 3 Servings
Main Ingredients
1.5 pounds beef roast, trimmed of excess fat
3 tablespoons olive oil
3 tablespoons whole-grain mustard
½ tablespoon rosemary, chopped
Salt and black pepper

Ingredients for the Sauce
2 cups red wine
1 cup flour, diluted in water
Salt and pepper

Directions
Rub the beef with olive oil, salt, pepper, mustard, and rosemary.
Seal the meat using any Vacuum Seal System that included bag
Then store it in the refrigerator for 15 minutes.
Now preheat the Oster Toaster oven and set timer to450 degrees F.
Take a broiling rack on the baking pan and put it on the broiling rack.
Cook according to personal preference, like for rare cook it for15 minutes, until tempura true is 130 degrees F.
For medium cook for 40 minutes until internal temperate is 145 degrees F.
Take a cooking pan and reduce the sauce ingredients to half.
Then slice and serve the beef with a drizzle of sauce.

Nutrition Facts
Servings: 3
Amount per serving
Calories   826
% Daily Value*
Total Fat 28.6g   37%
Saturated Fat 7.4g 37%
Cholesterol 203mg   68%
Sodium 158mg   7%

Total Carbohydrate 36.5g   13%
Dietary Fiber 1.4g 5%
Total Sugars 1.4g
Protein 73.2g

Ham Pastries

Preparation Time: 15 Minutes
Cooking Time: 20 Minutes
Yield: 4 Servings
Ingredients
4 slices of Serrano ham
8 ounces of cheese, goat cheese
8 sheets of puff pastry
 1 organic egg, lightly beaten

Directions
Preheat the Oster Toaster oven to 400 degrees F.
Turn on the bake function of the oven and press start.
Cut the cheese into 4 slices and wrap each slice over the ham.
 Layer and stretch the puff pastry sheet over a flat surface.
Cover it with flour, and use it to cover the chess covered ham, then take dough end toward the center and then roll and spread some egg at the end so the edges seal well.
Put it on to a greased baking pan.
Bake it in an Oster Toaster oven for 20 minutes.
Once the puff pastry is golden brown, let it rest for 5 minutes, then serve.

Nutrition Facts
Servings: 4
Amount per serving
Calories   730
% Daily Value*
Total Fat 52.3g   67%
Saturated Fat 31.1g   156%
Cholesterol 186mg   62%
Sodium 1573mg   68%
Total Carbohydrate 41.8g   15%
Dietary Fiber 2.4g 9%
Total Sugars 2.4g
Protein 26.2g

Thin Crust Pizza

Preparation Time: 15 Minutes
Cooking Time: 20 Minutes
Yield: 4 Servings
Ingredients
2.5 cups plain flour
2 teaspoons dried yeast
pinch of salt
¾ cup of warm water
4-6   teaspoons olive oil
1/4 cup of Plain flour, for kneading the dough
10 pepperonis
4 slices pizza cheese
4 black olives, chopped
1 cup pizza sauce
Directions
Mix dry yeast, flour, warm water, and salt in a bowl and then pour into blender
Add oil gradually and start the blender at low speed
Blend it until all oil is poured and the dough is formed. Let it sit for one hour.
Afterward, transfer the dough onto a flat work surface.
Knead the dough for 3 minutes using extra flour
Put the dough in a warm place to let it rise
Then roll the dough in pizza shape and add a topping of pizza sauce, pepperoni, cheese, and black olive
Bake it in the oven for 20 minutes at 400 degrees F. Once done, serve.

Nutrition Facts
Servings: 4
Amount per serving
Calories   800
% Daily Value*
Total Fat 21g   27%
Saturated Fat 9.7g 49%
Cholesterol 39mg 13%
Sodium 1069mg   46%
Total Carbohydrate 121.5g   44%
Dietary Fiber 5.1g 18%
Total Sugars 13.2g
Protein 28.6g

Beef Jerky

Preparation Time: 15 Minutes
Cooking Time:4 Hours
Yield: 4 Servings
Ingredients
2 pounds beef round steak, cut into 1 inch thick)
1 cup Worcestershire sauce
1 cup tamari sauce
½ cup brown sugar
1 tablespoon liquid smoke
2 tablespoons onion powder
1 tablespoon garlic powder
Salt and black pepper, to taste
1 teaspoon chili powder

Directions
Slice the meat into strips. Pound the meat to flatten them a bit.
Take a glass bowl and add all the listed ingredients with the meat strips.
Cover and refrigerate for 8 hours.
Preheat the Oster Toaster oven by turning on the convection bake function.
Put it on the lowest temperature.
Put a wire rack in a sheet pan, to collect dripping. Line the sheet with foil.
Put the meat strip on the wire rack. Let it cook for 4 hours. Then serve.

Nutrition Facts
Servings: 4
Amount per serving
Calories   665
% Daily Value*
Total Fat 20.3g   26%
Saturated Fat 7.1g 35%
Cholesterol 191mg   64%
Sodium 3326mg   145%
Total Carbohydrate 37g 13%
Dietary Fiber 1g   4%
Total Sugars 32.1g
Protein 77.4g

Maple-Glazed Sausages and Figs

Preparation Time: 15 Minutes
Cooking Time: 25 Minutes
Yield: 4 Servings
Ingredients
4 teaspoons of maple syrup
4 teaspoons of balsamic vinegar
8 meat sausage
8 ripe fresh figs
1 sweet onion
1 pound of Swiss chard
3 tablespoons of olive oil
Salt and black pepper, to taste
Directions
Preheat the Oster Toaster oven to 450 degrees F.
Take a bowl and mix maple syrup, balsamic vinegar.
Take foil baking sheet and layer figs and sausage in it.
Brush it with the maple mix and then roast it for 10 minutes.
Meanwhile, place the onion in a bowl and microwave it for 3 minutes.
Then add Swiss chard to onion, and microwave for 9 minutes.
Then add oil, salt, pepper and mix it well.
Take out sausage from the Oster Toaster oven and serve with onion and Swiss chard. Enjoy.

Nutrition Facts
Servings: 4
Amount per serving
Calories   467
% Daily Value*
Total Fat 31.2g   40%
Saturated Fat 8.6g 43%
Cholesterol 80mg 27%
Sodium 1668mg   73%
Total Carbohydrate 37.4g   14%
Dietary Fiber 6.2g 22%
Total Sugars 26.6g
Protein 17.6g

Chapter 3: Chicken & Poultry

Tandoori Chicken Wings

Preparation Time: 20 Minutes
Cooking Time: 20 Minutes
Yield: 4 Servings
Ingredients
2 pounds of chicken wings
3 tablespoons vegetable oil

Tandoori Sauce Ingredients
1 cup Greek yogurt
4 tablespoons mint leaves
1 teaspoon coriander, ground
1 teaspoon cumin, ground
2 teaspoons lemon juice
Salt and black pepper, to taste

Directions
Take a bowl and combine chicken wings with all the tandoori sauce ingredients. Let it refrigerate for 2 hours. Preheat the oven to 400 degrees F. Put the rack onto a baking tray and place the wings in it
Drizzle vegetable oil on top. Bake it for 20 minutes. Then serve.

Nutrition Facts
Servings: 4
Amount per serving
Calories   751
% Daily Value*
Total Fat 33.1g   42%
Saturated Fat 11.2g   56%
Cholesterol 217mg   72%
Sodium 296mg   13%
Total Carbohydrate 12.6g   5%
Dietary Fiber 0.4g 1%
Total Sugars 12.1g
Protein 96.1g

Chicken with Lemons And Garlic

Preparation Time: 20 Minutes
Cooking Time: 1-1/2 Hour
Yield: 4 Servings
Ingredients
2.5 pounds of chicken
2 tablespoons of olive oil
Salt and pepper, to taste
1 garlic clove
2 lemons, halved
2 fresh rosemary sprigs

Directions
Preheat the Oster Toaster oven to 425 degrees F.
Rub the chicken well with the olive oil
Then season it with salt, garlic, lemon halves, and pepper
Tuck the wingtips on the chicken back and tie the legs of the chicken tightly together.
Place the chicken in a small roasting pan.
Put the rosemary around the chicken.
Roast the chicken for 1-1/2 hours.
Once done, serve by craving into slices.

Nutrition Facts
Servings: 4
Amount per serving
Calories   489
% Daily Value*
Total Fat 15.6g   20%
Saturated Fat 3.4g 17%
Cholesterol 218mg   73%
Sodium 179mg   8%
Total Carbohydrate 0.3g 0%
Dietary Fiber 0g   0%
Total Sugars 0g
Protein 82.2g

BBQ Chicken Tenders

Preparation Time: 20 Minutes
Cooking Time: 12 Minutes
Yield: 2 Servings

Ingredients
10 ounces chicken tenders
Oil spray, for greasing
Salt and black pepper
1 tablespoon of barbeque flavor seasoning
Sauce Ingredients
2 tablespoons Dijon mustard
1 teaspoon pure honey

Directions
Preheat the Oster Toaster oven to 450 degrees F.
Take a cookie sheet and line it with foil.
Spray the foil with oil.
Season the chicken with salt, pepper, and BBQ seasoning.
Put the chicken tender onto a foil-lined tray.
Bake the chicken for 12 minutes.
Meanwhile, mix honey and mustard
Serve the chicken with prepared sauce as a dipping.

Nutrition Facts
Servings: 2
Amount per serving
Calories   282
% Daily Value*
Total Fat 11.4g   15%
Saturated Fat 3g   15%
Cholesterol 126mg   42%
Sodium 299mg   13%
Total Carbohydrate 0.9g 0%
Dietary Fiber 0.5g   2%
Total Sugars 0.1g
Protein 41.7g

Chicken Strips

Preparation Time: 20 Minutes
Cooking Time: 20 Minutes
Yield: 3 Servings
Ingredients
1.5 pounds of chicken tenders
Oil spray, for greasing
Salt and black pepper
1 teaspoon of Steak Seasoning
1 teaspoon of garlic and herb spice
1 cup ranch, side serving

Directions
Preheat the Oster Toaster oven to 450 degrees F.
Take a baking sheet and line it with foil.
Grease the foil with oil spray.
Season the chicken strips with salt, pepper, steak seasoning, and garlic herb spice.
Put the chicken strips onto the foil sheet.
Bake the chicken for 20 minutes at 450 degrees F.
Serve the chicken with ranch.

Nutrition Facts
Servings: 3
Amount per serving
Calories   488
% Daily Value*
Total Fat 17.9g   23%
Saturated Fat 4.7g 23%
Cholesterol 205mg   68%
Sodium 547mg   24%
Total Carbohydrate 12.4g   5%
Dietary Fiber 0.1g 0%
Total Sugars 2.5g
Protein 65.7g

Toaster Oven Corn Bread

Preparation Time: 10 Minutes
Cooking Time:2o Minutes
Yield: 6 Servings
Ingredients
1-1/2 cups Yellow Cornmeal
1 1-/4 cups Old Fashioned Quaker Oatmeal
Salt, pinch
1/3 cup Sugar
2 teaspoons of Baking Powder
1 cup of soy milk
1 small organic egg
1/3 cup Applesauce

Directions
Take a high-speed blender and pulse the oatmeal in the form of powder.
Add the oatmeal to the bowl and add baking powder, salt, sugar, egg, milk, and applesauce.
Mix all the ingredients well.
Pour this batter into a bread loaf pan.
Bake it for 20 minutes at 400 degrees F.
Once done, serve.

Nutrition Facts
Servings: 6
Amount per serving
Calories   179
% Daily Value*
Total Fat 2.6g   3%
Saturated Fat 0.5g 2%
Cholesterol 23mg 8%
Sodium 65mg   3%
Total Carbohydrate 36.2g   13%
Dietary Fiber 2.6g 9%
Total Sugars 14.5g
Protein 4.6g

Honey Mustard Chicken

Preparation Time: 25minutes
Cooking Time:40   Minutes
Yield:6 Servings
Ingredients
1 cup Dijon mustard
1/2 cup chopped pecans
1 cup honey
2 cups corn flakes
3 pounds of chicken thighs, skinless
Olive oil for drizzling
1 teaspoon cayenne pepper
Oil spray, for greasing
Directions
Take a baking tray and grease it with oil spray.
Take a food processor and pulse the corn flakes in it until crumbs.
Now in a small bowl, mix mustard and honey.
Coat the chicken with mustard and honey.
Take a separate bowl and mix cayenne pepper, crumbed cornflakes, and pecans. Put the chicken in a corn flakes mixture for fine coating.
Afterward, Put the breast pieces into the oil greased baking pan.
Top it with a drizzle of olive oil.
Bake at 375°F for 40 minutes in an Oster Toaster oven.
Once the reaches internal temperature reaches 170°F, the chicken is ready to be served。 Enjoy hot.

Nutrition Facts
Servings: 6
Amount per serving
Calories   694
% Daily Value*
Total Fat 21.8g   28%
Saturated Fat 5.2g 26%
Cholesterol 202mg   67%
Sodium 759mg   33%
Total Carbohydrate 57.2g   21%
Dietary Fiber 2.1g 8%
Total Sugars 47.4g
Protein 68.4g

Roasted Turkey Breast

Preparation Time: 20 Minutes
Cooking Time: 40 Minutes
Yield: 4 Servings
Ingredients
2 turkey breasts
2 stalks celery, cut into ¼ inch dice
2 cloves garlic, peeled
1 lemon, halved
1 or 2 sprigs each of fresh rosemary and fresh thyme
Chili powder
1 small onion, cut into ¼ inch dice
salt and pepper
3 small carrots cut into ¼ inch dice
1 1/2 cups chicken broth
Directions
Preheat the Oster Toaster oven to 450 degrees F.
Take a baking pan and place the vegetables in it.
Sprinkle vegetables with salt, black pepper, chili powder, and add garlic and herbs. Top the vegetables with turkey breast.
Drizzle the lemon juice on top of turkey breast pieces.
Set a timer for 25 minutes and reduce the temperature to 325 degrees F.
Pour the broth on the bottom of the pan.
Once the internal temperate reaches 180 degrees F, take out the baking pan and serve.

Nutrition Facts
Servings: 4
Amount per serving
Calories   857
% Daily Value*
Total Fat 32.6g   42%
Saturated Fat 9.2g 46%
Cholesterol 320mg   107%
Sodium 592mg   26%
Total Carbohydrate 6.4g 2%
Dietary Fiber 1.5g 5%
Total Sugars 3g
Protein 126.5g

Tex-Mex Chicken Quesadillas

Preparation Time: 15 Minutes
Cooking Time: 10 Minutes
Yield: 4 Servings
Ingredients
2 green onions, chopped
2 cups of chicken meat, shredded, skinless, rotisserie
1 1/2 cup Monterey Jack cheese, Shredded
1 pickled jalapeño, chopped
¼ cup cilantro leaves
4 flour tortillas, burrito-size
1/2 cup salsa Verde
1 cup sour cream, reduced-fat

Directions
Preheat the Oster Toaster oven to 400 degrees F.
Divide the chickens, cheese, jalapeno, green onion, and cilantro on one side
of each of the tortillas and fold the other half over it.
 Layer a foil on a toaster oven tray.
Put the tortilla wrap on it.
Bake it in the oven for 10 minutes.
Serve it with sour cream and salsa Verde.
Serve and enjoy.

Nutrition Facts
Servings: 4
Amount per serving
Calories   477
% Daily Value*
Total Fat 30.9g   40%
Saturated Fat 17.1g   86%
Cholesterol 125mg   42%
Sodium 503mg   22%
Total Carbohydrate 15.3g   6%
Dietary Fiber 1.9g 7%
Total Sugars 1.2g
Protein 34.4g

Eggs in Their Nests

Preparation Time: 15 Minutes
Cooking Time: 40-50 Minutes
Yield: 6 Servings
Ingredients
1.5 pounds of white potatoes, peeled and quartered
1 cup breadcrumbs
2 tablespoons of butter
4 long scallions, chopped
6 eggs
Salt, to taste
Directions
Boil water in a cooking pot and add potatoes.
Cook it until potatoes get soft.
Then drain potatoes in a bowl.
Mash the potatoes.
Preheat the Oster Toaster oven at 340 degrees F, by setting it to bake function.
In a skillet sauté onion in butter and add mashed potatoes.
Then add salt and bread crumbs.
Now cook it for 10 minutes, then transfer to muffin tins.
Divide the mixture equally among tins and then form a nest of potatoes.
 Bake it for 15 minutes in an Oster Toaster oven.
Afterward, remove it and then pour one egg into each nest.
Again put it in the Oster Toaster oven and cook for 10 more minutes using the bake function. Remove it from the oven. Serve.

Nutrition Facts
Servings: 6
Amount per serving
Calories   253
% Daily Value*
Total Fat 10.1g   13%
Saturated Fat 4.1g 20%
Cholesterol 174mg   58%
Sodium 255mg   11%
Total Carbohydrate 31.1g   11%
Dietary Fiber 3.5g 13%
Total Sugars 2.8g
Protein 9.9g

Eggs with Cream and Cheese

Preparation Time: 20 Minutes
Cooking Time: 15 Minutes
Yield: 2 Servings
Ingredients
½ cup cream
6 tablespoons cream cheese
1 teaspoon chives
1 tablespoon of Chinese onion
2 eggs
3 ½ ounces chicken
¼ cup spinach
1 tomato, chopped
¼ cup Gruyere cheese, cubed
Salt and pepper
Oil spray, for greasing
4 bread slices
Directions
Toast bread slices in an Oster Toaster Oven until golden brown from top.
Use a blender to blend cream, onions, chives, and cream cheese.
Transfer it to an oil greased heat-resistant bowl. In a bowl, whisk the eggs. Then add chicken. Add in remaining ingredients and mix.
Turn the Oster Toaster oven to bake egg and chicken mix, and cook it for 10 minutes at 375 degrees F,
Once done, serve with toast and cream cheese mixture.

Nutrition Facts
Servings: 2
Amount per serving
Calories   391
% Daily Value*
Total Fat 24.7g   32%
Saturated Fat 13.1g   66%
Cholesterol 261mg   87%
Sodium 374mg   16%
Total Carbohydrate 13.6g   5%
Dietary Fiber 0.9g 3%
Total Sugars 3.3g
Protein 28.5g

Chapter 4: Fish & Seafood

Scallops Sandwich

Preparation Time: 20 Minutes
Cooking Time: 10 Minutes
Yield: 2 Servings
Ingredients

1/3 cup pine nuts
2 Italian bread, thick and toasted
1 Yellow tomato, sliced
½ Romaine lettuces cut into strips
1 pound scallops

½ red bell pepper, diced
½ yellow bell pepper, diced
2 tablespoons cider vinegar
1/2 cup olive oil
Salt and black pepper, to taste

Directions

The first step is to toaster the bread in the Oster Toaster oven until the bread gets brown. Then set aside for further use.
Sear the scallops in 1 tablespoon of olive oil in a large skillet.
Now in a bowl mix oil, pepper, salt, vinegar, pine nut, and bell peppers.
Brush this liquid onto the bread.
Layer slices of tomato, lettuce, and scallops on top of bread slices.
Pour remaining dressing on top. Enjoy.

Nutrition Facts
Servings: 2
Amount per serving
Calories   1000
% Daily Value*
Total Fat 77.6g   99%
Saturated Fat 10.9g   55%
Cholesterol 80mg 27%
Sodium 570mg   25%
Total Carbohydrate 35g 13%
Dietary Fiber 1.8g 6%
Total Sugars 4.4g
Protein 46.1g

Blue Corn Enchiladas with Crabmeat

Preparation Time: 25 Minutes
Cooking Time: 25-30 Minutes
Yield: 4 Servings
Ingredients

2 green chilies, roasted and chopped
1/2 teaspoon red chili, dried
2 tablespoons of onion, chopped
2 cloves garlic, minced
2 tablespoons of butter
2 tablespoons of flour
1 tablespoon cumin, ground
1-1/3 cup dry white wine

1/3 cup sour cream
8 scallions, chopped, including greens
1.5 pounds of crabmeat, lumps
2.5 cups Monterey Jack cheese, grated
8 blue corn tortillas

Directions

Melt butter in skillet. Cook garlic and onion in it.
Then add green and red chilies, and stir in cumin and flour. Cook it for 3 minutes.
Then pour in the wine and simmer it for a few minutes until thickened.
Remove it from heat. Then add the sour cream.
Now add one cup of this mixture to the crab meat and one cup of cheese.
 Soft the tortillas with a damp cloth and then microwave it for a few seconds
Put a few tablespoons of the crab mixture on each of the tortillas.
Then roll the tortilla
Prepare the tortilla on the dish and then pour the remaining prepared sauce on top and the remaining cheese.
Bake it in the Oster Toaster oven for 15 minutes, at 350 degrees F. Serve.

Nutrition Facts
Servings: 4
Amount per serving
Calories   705
% Daily Value*
Total Fat 33.8g   43%
Saturated Fat 20.2g   101%
Cholesterol 121mg   40%
Sodium 1893mg   82%
Total Carbohydrate 56.7g   21%
Dietary Fiber 5.1g   18%
Total Sugars 12.9g
Protein 35.1g

Shrimp Casserole

Preparation Time: 20 Minutes
Cooking Time: 30 Minutes
Yield: 4 Servings
Ingredients

2 tablespoons organic butter
4 tablespoons bread crumbs
2.5 pounds shrimp
2 tablespoons olive oil
2 small onions, chopped
2 celery ribs, chopped
3 garlic cloves, minced
4 cups chicken broth

Salt and black pepper, to taste
1 cup converted rice
1 tablespoon parsley, chopped
1 tablespoon lemon juice
1 teaspoon lemon zest
1 cup sour cream
½ cup Parmesan cheese, grated

Directions

Take a casserole dish and butter it well then sprinkle bread crumbs evenly.
Preheat the Oster Toaster Oven to 325 degrees F.
De-vain and cut the shrimps.
Take a saucepan and heat olive oil in it over medium flame.
Cook the onions, celery, salt, pepper, and garlic and add rice
Pour in the broth and allow it to boil.
Remove it from the heat.
Then add lemon juice, zest, cream, parsley.
Then put it into a casserole dish.
Sprinkle the parmesan cheese on top.
Cover the dish with aluminum foil.
Bake it in Oster Toaster Oven at 325 degrees F for 20 minutes.
Remove the foil after 20 minutes of cooking
Cook for 10 more minutes and serve it hot.

Nutrition Facts
Servings: 4
Amount per serving
Calories   914
% Daily Value*
Total Fat 37.7g   48%
Saturated Fat 18.2g   91%
Cholesterol 658mg   219%

Sodium 1841mg   80%
Total Carbohydrate 54.8g   20%
Dietary Fiber 1.8g 6%
Total Sugars 2.9g
Protein 85.1g

Toaster Oven Pesto Salmon

Preparation Time: 20 Minutes
Cooking Time: 15-20 Minutes
Yield: 3 Servings
Ingredients
1.5 pounds of salmon filet, cut into 4 pieces
2 tablespoons pesto, thawed
4 tablespoons toasted pine nuts, optional
2 lemons, halved

Directions
Take a toaster oven baking dish and cover it with foil.
Coat the foil with oil spray.
Put the salmon fillets, skin-side down, on the oven pan.
Squeeze one lemon juice on top of salmon.
Let it marinate for 20 minutes.
Meanwhile preheat the toaster oven broiler.
Now put the pesto over each salmon.
Place salmon on baking dish for baking.
Bake salmon in the Oster Toaster oven for 10-15 minutes.
Broil for few minutes for crispy outside.
Once done, top each salmon with pine nuts and lemon slices.

Nutrition Facts
Servings: 3
Amount per serving
Calories   338
% Daily Value*
Total Fat 14.2g   18%
Saturated Fat 1.4g 7%
Cholesterol 3mg   1%
Sodium 457mg   20%
Total Carbohydrate 11.7g   4%
Dietary Fiber 0.6g 2%
Total Sugars 1.1g
Protein 2.6g

Crab Tarts

Preparation Time: 30 Minutes
Cooking Time: 20 Minutes
Yield: 4 Servings
Ingredients

2 tablespoons olive oil
1 small onion, chopped
2 garlic cloves, minced
4 tablespoons dry white wine
2 eggs, small
4 ounces cream

8 ounces surimi crab meat
2 ounces Parmesan cheese, grated
4 tablespoons parsley, chopped
2 pinch of nutmeg, freshly ground
Salt and black pepper to taste
1 roll of pastry dough

Directions

Preheat the Oster Toaster oven to 350 degrees F.
Set it to bake function. Take a skillet and add olive oil.
Cook onion for 5 minutes then add garlic and cook until aroma comes.
Then add the wine and cook until it reduces to half.
Whisk egg in a bowl and start adding crab meat, cream, nutmeg, cheese, onion mix from skillet, salt, pepper, and parsley.,
Now make a tart bottom, for that put the dough on a flat surface
Now use a rolling pin to roll it and then cut it into circular shapes.
Take the tart mold and grease it with oil spray.
Put the circular dough in molds, and bake in the Oster Toaster oven for 10 minutes
Then remove it from the oven and then top the dough with crab filling.
Bake again for 10 minutes and serve.

Nutrition Facts
Servings: 4
Amount per serving
Calories   329
% Daily Value*
Total Fat 20.2g   26%
Saturated Fat 7.9g 40%
Cholesterol 120mg   40%
Sodium 575mg   25%
Total Carbohydrate 22.2g   8%
Dietary Fiber 0.7g 3%
Total Sugars 8.2g
Protein 13.6g

Grilled Scallops With Butter

Preparation Time: 10 Minutes
Cooking Time: 12 Minutes
Yield: 3 Servings
Ingredients

12 shells with scallop, fan-shaped
2 tablespoons butter
2 tablespoons parsley, chopped
½ onion, chopped
1 garlic clove, minced

1 teaspoon green pepper, chopped
½ teaspoon lemon zest
1 cup bread grated
2 teaspoons of olive oil
Salt and pepper

Directions

Clean the scallop shells well and remove the coral.
Take a bowl and mix the butter, salt, black pepper, onion, garlic, green pepper, and parsley, and lemon zest.
Now, in a skillet, heat olive oil and sauté the bread until brown.
Then make crumbs of bread.
Add the scallops to the baking tray and add the buttered parsley mix.
Sprinkle the grated bread crumbs.
Transfer it to the Oster Toaster oven and turn on the bake function, and cook until golden brown.
Serve and enjoy.

Nutrition Facts
Servings: 3
Amount per serving
Calories   908
% Daily Value*
Total Fat 48.5g   62%
Saturated Fat 26.5g   133%
Cholesterol 280mg   93%
Sodium 982mg   43%
Total Carbohydrate 27.5g   10%
Dietary Fiber 4.9g 17%
Total Sugars 0.9g
Protein 91.9g

Almond Crusted Fish Fillet

Preparation Time: 15 Minutes
Cooking Time: 15 Minutes
Yield: 2 Servings
Ingredients

2 fish fillets
2 ounces of bread crumbs, grated
2 ounces of Parmesan cheese
2 ounces almonds, grounded

1 stick of butter
Salt and black pepper, to taste
Oil spray, for greasing

Ingredients for The Sauce

1 cup heavy cream
½ lemons

1/3 cup white wine

Directions

Take a food processor and mix bread crumbs, parmesan cheese, butter, and almonds.

Blend it to form a paste.

Wrap it in a plastic wrap in the shape and size of the fish fillet.

Afterward, grease a baking pan with oil spray.

Put the fish fillet onto the pan, skin side down, and season it with salt and pepper.

Take out the wrap rectangular shape and put it on top of the fillet.

Bake it in the Oster Toaster oven for 10 minutes at 390 degrees F.

Meanwhile, cook cream in white wine and reduce it to half, using a cooking pan. Pour it over cooked fillet and enjoy it.

Nutrition Facts
Servings: 2
Amount per serving
Calories   1226
% Daily Value*
Total Fat 101.2g   130%
Saturated Fat 50.9g   255%
Cholesterol 255mg   85%
Sodium 1305mg   57%
Total Carbohydrate 45.7g   17%
Dietary Fiber 5.3g 19%
Total Sugars 3.4g
Protein 34g

Salmon Wontons with Ginger

Preparation Time: 25 Minutes
Cooking Time: 20 Minutes
Yield: 4 Servings
Ingredients
8 tablespoons soy sauce
1/3 cup fresh ginger, minced
1/4 cup rice vinegar
4 tablespoons honey
1/2 pound salmon, diced
3/4 cup onion, chopped
1/4 cup scallions, chopped

1 large egg
2 teaspoon garlic, minced
1/3 teaspoon red crushed chilies
Salt to taste
12 ounces package wonton wrappers
Vegetable oil for frying

Directions
Take a bowl and mix half of the soy sauce,2 tablespoons of ginger, honey, and vinegar

In a separate bowl combine salmon, onions, egg, remaining ginger, garlic, scallions, chilies, and remaining soy sauce.

Place wonton wrappers on a flat surface and brush the edges with water.

Place a large teaspoon of salmon filling in the center and fold the wonton

Seal edges Put the wonton on waxed paper. Repeat with all the wrappers.

Preheat Oster Toaster Oven to 250 degrees F.

Heat oil in a skillet and add wonton

Fry until golden, 4 minutes per side.Then transfer to baking pan

Bake in the Oster Toaster oven for 5 minutes.

Serve wontons with the honey-soy sauce.

Nutrition Facts
Servings: 4
Amount per serving
Calories   998
% Daily Value*
Total Fat 61g   78%
Saturated Fat 11.9g   60%
Cholesterol 79mg 26%
Sodium 2391mg   104%
Total Carbohydrate 87.4g   32%
Dietary Fiber 3.6g 13%
Total Sugars 19.7g
Protein 25.8g

Salmon Sandwich and Yogurt Dressing

Preparation Time: 20 Minutes
Cooking Time: 7 Minutes
Yield: 1 Serving
Ingredients

1 large piece of flatbread
4 ounces of salmon fillets
1/2 teaspoon thyme dried
1/2 teaspoon sesame seeds
1/2 cucumber, peeled
2 tablespoons of yogurt

1 zucchini cut into pieces
1 tablespoon pine nuts
1/2 teaspoon dried oregano
2 tablespoons olive oil
Salt and black pepper, to taste

Directions

Cut the salmon fillet into 1 inch thick slices.
Season the salmon fillet with olive oil, thyme, salt, pepper, and sesame seed.
Layer the slices flat toward the center of the bread.
Put the bread in the toaster oven.
Broil for 4 minutes.
Meanwhile, combine yogurt and cucumber and season it with salt and black pepper.
Take out the bread and then layer zucchini, oregano, salt, black pepper, and pine nut in a foil baking tray.
 broil for 3 minutes.
Once it's done, serve the flatbread with zucchini and yogurt dressings.
Enjoy.

Nutrition Facts
Servings: 1
Amount per serving
Calories   625
% Daily Value*
Total Fat 45.1g   58%
Saturated Fat 6g   30%
Cholesterol 52mg   17%
Sodium 305mg   13%
Total Carbohydrate 30.2g   11%
Dietary Fiber 5.8g   21%
Total Sugars 8.4g
Protein 31.6g
Chapter 5: Desserts and Snacks

Toaster Oven Coconut Salmon

Preparation Time: 20 Minutes
Cooking Time: 15-20 Minutes
Yield: 3 Servings
Ingredients
1.5 pounds of salmon, filets
Salt and black pepper, to taste
½ cup coconut flakes
1 cup Panko bread crumbs
2 lemons, halved

Directions
Take a baking sheet and cover it with aluminum foil.
Coat the foil with oil spray.
Take a bowl and add Panko crumbs, salt, pepper and coconut flakes.
Season salmon with lemon juice, salt and black pepper.
Coat the salmon filets with crumb mixture from both sides.
Preheat the toaster oven broiler.
Bake salmon in the Oster Toaster oven for 10-15 minutes.
Broil for few minutes for crispy outside.
Serve hot.

Nutrition Facts
Servings: 2
Amount per serving
Calories   820
% Daily Value*
Total Fat 13.3g   17%
Saturated Fat 6.6g 33%
Cholesterol 0mg   0%
Sodium 1312mg   57%
Total Carbohydrate 89.9g   33%
Dietary Fiber 4.2g 15%
Total Sugars 4.6g
Protein 7.9g

Chapter 5: Desserts

Eggs Pound Cake

Preparation Time: 30 Minutes
Cooking Time: 80 Minutes
Yield: 4 Servings
Ingredients

3 sticks of solid butter
2 ½ cups brown sugar, granulated
6 large eggs
3 cups All-Purpose flour

1 tablespoon of baking powder
Pinch of salt
¾ cup almond milk

Directions
Preheat the Oster Toaster oven to 350 degrees F.
Grease a cake pan with oil spray and dust a little amount of the flour on the bottom.
Add butter to the bowl and use a hand beater to mix the butter with sugar until fluffy and creamy. Then add the eggs and keep on mixing.
Pour in almond milk and gently stir the ingredients together.
 Dump in the flour generously and slowly.
Then add salt and baking soda. Mix all the things well.
Spoon prepared batter into greased pan.
Bake in the oster oven for 80 minutes. Let it cool and serve. Enjoy

Nutrition Facts
Servings: 4
Amount per serving
Calories   1050
% Daily Value*
Total Fat 35.6g   46%
Saturated Fat 22.5g   112%
Cholesterol 324mg   108%
Sodium 181mg   8%
Total Carbohydrate 165.3g   60%
Dietary Fiber 3.6g 13%
Total Sugars 90.3g
Protein 20.3g

Chocolate Chip Cookies

Preparation Time: 20 Minutes
Cooking Time: 15 Minutes
Yield: 6 Servings
Ingredients
2 sticks butter
⅔ cup soft light brown sugar
½ cup granulated sugar
2 teaspoons vanilla extract
2 teaspoons of almond extract
1 egg yolk
1 egg
2 cups flour, all-Purpose
1 tablespoon of baking soda
1 cup of chocolate chips
Directions
Preheat the Oster Toaster oven to 325 degrees F
Line a baking sheet with parchment paper and set aside for further.
Mix butter with both sugars in a mixing bowl and combine until softened
Add vanilla and almond extract along with the egg and egg yolk, and
continue the mixing
Then add in flour slowly and add baking soda.
Then add a chocolate chip and turn off the mixer.
 Drop the prepared dough onto the prepared baking sheets.
And bake it in the Oster Toaster oven for 15 minutes.

Nutrition Facts
Servings: 6
Amount per serving
Calories   630
% Daily Value*
Total Fat 33.9g   43%
Saturated Fat 20.3g   101%
Cholesterol 147mg   49%
Sodium 882mg   38%
Total Carbohydrate 76.6g   28%
Dietary Fiber 1.3g 5%
Total Sugars 42.6g
Protein 6.5g

Cake with Coconut Glaze

Preparation Time: 30 Minutes
Cooking Time: 40 Minutes
Yield: 6 Servings
Main Ingredients
2.5 cups nut oil
1 cup brown sugar
⅔ Cup coconut cream
3 eggs, whisked
2 cup almond flour
2 large carrots, grated
2 teaspoon baking powder
12 teaspoon baking soda
2 teaspoons cinnamon, ground
2 teaspoons allspice, ground
Pinch of sea salt
Oil spray, for greasing

Glaze Ingredients
2 cups coconut flakes, toasted
½ cup coconut cream
 1 /2 cup icing sugar

Directions
Preheat the Oster Toaster oven to 350 degrees F.
Grease a Bundt cake pan with oil spray.
 Take a blender and pulse together cream, egg, and sugar.
Secure the lid and blend for 20 seconds.
 Now add the remaining ingredients to the blender jar and mix well.
Blend it for 20 seconds
Pour this mixture into the pan
Bake it in the oster toaster oven for 40 minutes
Meanwhile, prepare the glaze and blend all the glaze ingredients in a blender
Place all ingredients into the blender jar.
Pour this glaze over the cooked cake
Serve and enjoy

Nutrition Facts

Servings: 6
Amount per serving
Calories   1193
% Daily Value*
Total Fat 112.5g   144%
Saturated Fat 29.9g   149%
Cholesterol 82mg 27%
Sodium 2626mg   114%
Total Carbohydrate 47.5g   17%
Dietary Fiber 5.2g 18%
Total Sugars 39g
Protein 6.9g

Parmesan Crackers

Preparation Time: 20 Minutes
Cooking Time: 12 Minutes
Yield: 4 Servings
Ingredients
1 -1/2 cup plain flour
½ cup parmesan cheese, grated
1 stick of butter
½ cup thickened cream

Directions
Preheat the Oster Toaster oven to 400 degrees F.
Grease the baking tray with oil and place the baking paper in it.
Take a food processor and add flour, cheese, and butter.
Secure lid and blend on medium.
Add cream and blender for 30 seconds.
Transfer the mixture to the flat surface.
 Form the balls of the dough.
Roll the dough and use pastry cute to cut it into squares.
Place square on to the baking tray.
Bake it in the Oster Toaster oven for 12 minutes.
One done, serve.
Enjoy.

Nutrition Facts
Servings: 4
Amount per serving
Calories   449
% Daily Value*
Total Fat 33.8g   43%
Saturated Fat 21.5g   108%
Cholesterol 81mg 27%
Sodium 427mg   19%
Total Carbohydrate 25.2g   9%
Dietary Fiber 0.8g 3%
Total Sugars 0.5g
Protein 12.7g

Banana Bread

Preparation Time: 30 Minutes
Cooking Time: 40 Minutes
Yield: 6 Servings
Ingredients
6 medium ripe bananas
4 eggs, whisked
1/3 cup coconut oil
3 tablespoons honey
1 tablespoon lemon juice
1 teaspoon vanilla extract
2.5 cups almond meal
¼ cup ground flaxseed
2 teaspoons baking soda
1 teaspoon ground allspice
Directions
Preheat the Oster Toaster oven to 320 degrees F
Take a loaf pan and grease it with oil spray.
 Add three bananas, honey, coconut oil, lemon juice, vanilla, and eggs in a blender and pulse to form a smooth paste
 Add these wet ingredients to the bowl.
Then add almond meal, baking soda, flaxseed, and allspice
Mix and combine well.
Pour this mixture into a prepared pan and top with slices of remaining bananas.
 Bake it for 40 minutes Once done, serve

Nutrition Facts
Servings: 6
Amount per serving
Calories   540
% Daily Value*
Total Fat 36.3g   47%
Saturated Fat 13.1g   66%
Cholesterol 109mg   36%
Sodium 464mg   20%
Total Carbohydrate 46.1g   17%
Dietary Fiber 9.3g 33%
Total Sugars 24.7g
Protein 14g

Carrot Bread

Preparation Time: 20 Minutes
Cooking Time: 50 Minutes
Yield: 8 Servings
Ingredients

1-1/3 cups all-purpose flour
1 tablespoon baking soda
1 teaspoon cinnamon
1 cup pecans
2 eggs

Salt, to taste
1 cup of vegetable oil
3/4 cup brown sugar
1 tablespoon vanilla extract
2 cups carrots cut small pieces

Directions

Preheat the Oster Toaster oven to 375 degrees F.
Grease a loaf pan.
Take a bowl and mix cinnamon, salt, baking soda, and flour.
Then add pecans.
Now in a blender blend eggs, vanilla, sugar, and oil.
Process it until smooth.
Next, add carrots to the blender and process again.
Add this mixture over dry ingredients in a bowl and mix well.
Now put this mixture into a loaf pan and bake in the Oster Toaster oven for 45-55 minutes
One toothpick comes out clean serve

Nutrition Facts
Servings: 8
Amount per serving
Calories   511
% Daily Value*
Total Fat 41g   53%
Saturated Fat 7g   35%
Cholesterol 41mg 14%
Sodium 544mg   24%
Total Carbohydrate 32.8g   12%
Dietary Fiber 3.6g 13%
Total Sugars 16.4g
Protein 5.3g

Chocolate Brownies

Preparation Time: 20 Minutes
Cooking Time: 25 Minutes
Yield: 4 Servings
Ingredients
8 ounces of dark chocolate, dairy-free and melted
¼ cup of vegetable oil
1-1/2 cups flour, self-rising
¼ cup of cocoa powder
1/3 cup brown sugar
1 cup almond milk
1 cup macadamia nuts, chopped
Oil spray, for greasing

Directions
Preheat the Oster Toaster oven to 350°F.
Grease a baking pan or cake pan with oil spray.
Put the chocolate with oil in the blender
Blend until smooth
 Then add all the listed ingredients excluding macadamias
Pour the smooth mixture into a prepared baking pan and top with nuts
Bake it in the Oster Toaster oven for 25 minutes
Once it's done, serve.

Nutrition Facts
Servings: 4
Amount per serving
Calories   975
% Daily Value*
Total Fat 71.3g   91%
Saturated Fat 31.7g   158%
Cholesterol 13mg 4%
Sodium 61mg   3%
Total Carbohydrate 80.3g   29%
Dietary Fiber 8.6g 31%
Total Sugars 44.6g
Protein 12.6g

Chocolate Chip Cookies

Preparation Time: 20 Minutes
Cooking Time: 10 Minutes
Yield: 6 Servings
Ingredients

½ cup brown sugar
½ cup of coconut oil
¼ cup granulated sugar
1 teaspoons vanilla extract
1 egg, whisked
1-1/2 cups brown rice flour

¼ cup cornstarch
1 tablespoon arrowroot
1 teaspoon baking soda
½ teaspoon xanthan gum
Sea salt, pinch
• 1-1/2 cups dark chocolate chips

Directions

Preheat the Oster Toaster ovine to 350 degrees F.
Grease baking trays with baking paper.
 Combine oil, sugars, and vanilla in a food processor and blend
Then add egg and blend it for 2 minutes
Then add corn starch, flour, arrowroot, salt, baking soda, and xanthan gum.
Combine all the ingredients well.
Then mix in chocolate chip cookies
Put about large tablespoon size ball on a baking tray and bake it for 10 minutes
Once done, serve and enjoy.

Nutrition Facts
Servings: 6
Amount per serving
Calories   588
% Daily Value*
Total Fat 32.1g   41%
Saturated Fat 24.8g   124%
Cholesterol 37mg 12%
Sodium 260mg   11%
Total Carbohydrate 70.5g   26%
Dietary Fiber 2.7g 10%
Total Sugars 42.1g
Protein 6.1g

Chocolate Chip Cheesecake

Preparation Time: 20 Minutes
Cooking Time: 30 Minutes
Yield: 6 Servings
Ingredients
30 chocolate cookies
2 tablespoons melted butter
10 ounces of cream cheese
1 cup of condensed milk
4 egg whites
1 tablespoon vanilla extract
1 cup of chocolate chips
Oil spray, for greasing

Directions
Preheat the Oster Toaster oven to 375 degrees F.
Use a round cake mold and grease it with oil spray.
Use a food processor and crush the chocolate cookie in it.
Then add melted butter and mix well
Then layer it to cake mold to form a crust.
Now prepare the filling and add all the remaining ingredients in a blender
Pour the mixture and top the crust with it
Put the cake mold in the Oster Toaster oven and then bake it for 30 minutes.
Afterward, let it get cool and refrigerate it for 4 hours
Serve and enjoy.

Nutrition Facts
Servings: 6
Amount per serving
Calories   570
% Daily Value*
Total Fat 35.2g   45%
Saturated Fat 22.3g   112%
Cholesterol 88mg 29%
Sodium 308mg   13%
Total Carbohydrate 52.1g   19%
Dietary Fiber 1g   3%
Total Sugars 42.7g
Protein 12.7g

Sea Salt And Bacon Cookies

Preparation Time: 25 Minutes
Cooking Time: 12 Minutes
Yield: 8 Servings
Ingredients
2.5 cups of all-purpose flour
½ tablespoons baking soda
2.5 cups dark chocolate chips
12 strips of cooked bacon Strips
1.5 cups butter
1 cup brown sugar, granulated
3 eggs
2 teaspoons vanilla extract
Sea salt, for sprinkling
Directions
Preheat the Oster Toaster oven to 350 degrees F.
Take the oven tray and line it with baking paper.
In a bowl mix flour, chocolate chip, and baking soda.
Use a blender to mix butter with sugar, vanilla, and eggs.
Transfer it to the flour bowl and mix the ingredients well.
Roll into round shapes and place them on an oven tray.
Sprinkle sea salt on top.
Bake it in the oven for 12 minutes, until golden.
Once cool remove the cookies.
Serve and enjoy.

Nutrition Facts
Servings: 8
Amount per serving
Calories   808
% Daily Value*
Total Fat 53.3g   68%
Saturated Fat 29.4g   147%
Cholesterol 153mg   51%
Sodium 840mg   37%
Total Carbohydrate 75.9g   28%
Dietary Fiber 2.6g 9%
Total Sugars 38g
Protein

Chapter 6: Vegan & Vegetarian

Kale Chips

Preparation Time: 10 Minutes
Cooking Time: 5 Minutes
Yield: 2 Servings
Ingredients
2 cups of kale leaves
2 teaspoons of olive oil
Sea salt, to taste
1 teaspoon of lemon peel, grated

Directions
Preheat the Oster Toaster oven to 320 degrees F.
Put the baking rack inside it.
 Place kale leaves on a cookie sheet.
Drizzle olive oil on top and season with lemon grate and salt.
 Put cookie sheet on baking rack and bake at 5 minutes.
Rotate pieces to cook form bake after 2 minutes.
Once done, serve.

Nutrition Facts
Servings: 2
Amount per serving
Calories   74
% Daily Value*
Total Fat 4.7g   6%
Saturated Fat 0.7g 3%
Cholesterol 0mg   0%
Sodium 146mg   6%
Total Carbohydrate 7.2g 3%
Dietary Fiber 1.1g 4%
Total Sugars 0.1g
 Protein 2g

Roasted Asparagus in a Toaster Oven

Preparation Time: 20 Minutes
Cooking Time: 15 Minutes
Yield: 3 Servings
Ingredients
15 ounces asparagus, rinsed
Sea salt, to taste
1/6 teaspoon ground black pepper
4 teaspoons coconut oil, melted

Directions
Preheat the Oster Toaster oven to400 degrees F.
Take a roasting pan and grease it with one teaspoon of coconut oil.
Remove the asparagus ends and chop to pull back asparagus until then snap.
 Drizzle coconut oil over asparagus and season it with salt and black pepper.
Place it on a roasting pan and bake it in the oven for 15 minutes.
Once done, serve.

Nutrition Facts
Servings: 3
Amount per serving
Calories   81
% Daily Value*
Total Fat 6.2g   8%
Saturated Fat 5.3g 26%
Cholesterol 0mg   0%
Sodium 81mg   4%
Total Carbohydrate 5.6g 2%
Dietary Fiber 3g   11%
Total Sugars 2.7g
Protein 3.1g

Vegetable Stew

Preparation Time: 20 Minutes
Cooking Time: 40 Minutes
Yield: 2   Servings
Ingredients
4 tablespoons olive oil
1 onion, chopped
1/3 pound fresh mushrooms, sliced
2 carrots, coarsely chopped
3 large russet potatoes cut into quarters
1 stalk of celery, chopped
2 cloves garlic, minced
2 tablespoons all-purpose flour
Salt and pepper to taste

Directions
Preheat the Oster Toaster oven to 450 degrees F.
Take a bowl and add mushrooms, salt, pepper, onions, potatoes, celery, carrots, and garlic on a roasting pan.
Drizzle the olive oil on top.
Place it in the Oster Toaster oven and bake for 35 minutes.
Stir it occasionally.
Add two tablespoon of almond flour to vegetable and coated let it bake it for 5 more minutes. Once done, serve

Nutrition Facts
Servings: 2
Amount per serving
Calories   720
% Daily Value*
Total Fat 28.9g   37%
Saturated Fat 4.2g 21%
Cholesterol 0mg   0%
Sodium 89mg   4%
Total Carbohydrate 107.8g   39%
Dietary Fiber 17.1g 61%
Total Sugars 13.2g
Protein 13.9g

Roasted Zucchini

Preparation Time: 20 Minutes
Cooking Time: 12 Minutes
Yield: 3 Servings
Ingredients
2 large zucchinis, half lengthwise
Salt and black pepper
1 teaspoon garlic cloves, minced
1/2 teaspoon or dried thyme
Oil spray
2 teaspoons of olive oil

Directions
Preheat the Oster Toaster oven to 400 degrees F.
Take a roasting pan and grease it with oil spray,
Out zucchini in bowl and add salt, pepper, garlic cloves, thyme and olive oil.
Layer it on a roasting pan and bake it in the oven for 12 minutes, using convection bake function.
Once done, serve.

Nutrition Facts
Servings: 2
Amount per serving
Calories   96
% Daily Value*
Total Fat 5.5g   7%
Saturated Fat 0.8g 4%
Cholesterol 0mg   0%
Sodium 33mg   1%
Total Carbohydrate 11.3g   4%
Dietary Fiber 3.6g   13%
Total Sugars 5.6g
Protein 4g

Oster Toaster Oven Broccoli

Preparation Time: 20 Minutes
Cooking Time: 10 Minutes
Yield: 2   Servings
Ingredients
12 ounces Broccoli Crowns
3 cloves Garlic, peeled and thinly sliced
2 tablespoons Olive Oil, or avocado oil
Salt and black pepper, to taste
¼ teaspoon Red Pepper Flakes, optional
1/2 Lemon

Directions
Preheat the Oster Toaster oven to 400 degrees F.
Oil grease a baking tray.
Mix broccoli, salt, black pepper, red pepper, oil, and garlic in a bowl.
Toss broccoli well and then layer it on a baking tray
Put the baking tray in the Oster Toaster oven
Bake it for 10 to 16 serve with a squeeze of lemon

Nutrition Facts
Servings: 2
Amount per serving
Calories   26
% Daily Value*
Total Fat 1.8g   2%
Saturated Fat 0.4g 2%
Cholesterol 0mg   0%
Sodium 1mg   0%
Total Carbohydrate 2.4g 1%
Dietary Fiber 0.8g 3%
Total Sugars 0.1g
Protein 0.5g

Mix Roasted Vegetables

Preparation Time: 20 Minutes
Cooking Time: 15-20 Minutes
Yield: 4   Servings
Ingredients
1 pound of mixed vegetables
2 tablespoons Olive Oil
Salt and black pepper

Directions
Preheat the Oster Toaster oven to 425 degrees F.
layer the vegetables on the baking sheet.
Brush it with olive oil
Season it with salt and black pepper.
Roast in the preheated oven for 15 minutes.
Bake for few more minutes, until the desired tenderness achieve,
Serve and enjoy.

Nutrition Facts
Servings: 4
Amount per serving
Calories   128
% Daily Value*
Total Fat 7.2g   9%
Saturated Fat 1g   5%
Cholesterol 0mg   0%
Sodium 307mg   13%
Total Carbohydrate 14.9g   5%
Dietary Fiber 5g   18%
Total Sugars 3.5g
Protein 3.2g

Toaster Oven Red Potatoes

Preparation Time: 20 Minutes
Cooking Time: 30 Minutes
Yield: 4 Servings
Ingredients
4 red potatoes, quartered
1 red onion, quartered
¼ cup vegetable broth
Salt and black pepper, to taste
2 tablespoons of fresh thyme
2 tablespoons of Olive oil

Directions
Preheat the Oster Toaster oven to 400 degrees F.
Take a shallow baking tray and put onions and potatoes on it
Then add salt, pepper, olive oil, thyme, and broth
Cover it with aluminum foil and bake in oster oven for 20-30 minute
Once done, serve.

Nutrition Facts
Servings: 4
Amount per serving
Calories   225
% Daily Value*
Total Fat 7.4g   10%
Saturated Fat 1.1g 6%
Cholesterol 0mg   0%
Sodium 48mg   2%
Total Carbohydrate 37.5g   14%
Dietary Fiber 4.8g 17%
Total Sugars 3.4g
Protein 4.5g

Spice Glaze Potatoes

Preparation Time: 20 Minutes
Cooking Time: 18 Minutes
Yield: 2 Servings
4 tablespoons butter, melted
1/3 teaspoon ginger powder, ground
1/4 teaspoon nutmeg
1/3 teaspoon cinnamon
1/3 teaspoon cumin
3 sweet potatoes
Cayenne pepper, to taste

Directions
Preheat the Oster Toaster oven to 400 degrees F.
Take a bowl and add butter to it.
Melt butter in the microwave for few seconds
Add salt, cumin, ginger powder, nutmeg, cinnamon, cayenne pepper, and melted butter and mix it well
Now toss the potatoes in melted butter.
Later the potatoes on a baking tray and then bake in the Oster Toaster oven for 18 minutes
Once, done serve.

Nutrition Facts
Servings: 2
Amount per serving
Calories   474
% Daily Value*
Total Fat 23.6g   30%
Saturated Fat 14.8g   74%
Cholesterol 61mg 20%
Sodium 185mg   8%
Total Carbohydrate 63.6g   23%
Dietary Fiber 9.6g 34%
Total Sugars 1.3g
Protein 3.8g

Chocolate Tart

Preparation Time: 20 Minutes
Cooking Time: 20 Minutes
Yield: 4 Servings
Ingredients
7 ounces chocolate, chopped
1/3 cup brewed espresso
1-1/3 cup butter
1/3 cup white sugar
6 egg yolks
6 egg whites
1/2 cup pastry flour
Directions
Preheat the Oster Toaster Oven to 350 degrees F.
Heat butter with coffee in a microwave and mix well
Then add chocolate and combine the ingredients.
Take a separate bowl and whip ¼ cup of white sugar along with egg yolks to form ribbons.
In a separate bowl whip remaining sugar with egg white until soft pea form on top. Combine all these three mixtures in one big bowl.
Then add pastry flour.
Mix it all well. Transfer it to the cake pan.
Bake it in the Oster Toaster oven for 15-20 minutes
Afterward, let it get cool, and then return to the Oster Toaster oven and bake until the exterior is firm. Serve and enjoy.

Nutrition Facts
Servings: 4
Amount per serving
Calories   884
% Daily Value*
Total Fat 72.6g   93%
Saturated Fat 38.7g   193%
Cholesterol 442mg   147%
Sodium 391mg   17%
Total Carbohydrate 53.5g   19%
Dietary Fiber 2.9g 10%
Total Sugars 38.5g
Protein 15g

White Corn Cookies

Preparation Time: 20 Minutes
Cooking Time: 20 Minutes
Yield: 4 Servings
Ingredients
10 tablespoons butter
3/4 cup honey
2 egg whites
2/3 cup flour, all-purpose
3/4 cup sugar, superfine
3/4 cup white cornmeal

Directions
Preheat the Oster Toaster oven to 350 degrees F.
Take a bowl and combine sugar, cornmeal, and flour
Take a separate bowl and mix butter, eggs, with honey until no lumps remain.
Then add dry ingredients to wet ingredients
Use a hand Mixer to it until smooth
Grease a cookie sheet with oil spray.
Drop a heaping tablespoon of mixture on the cookie sheets.
Bake until golden.

Nutrition Facts
Servings: 4
Amount per serving
Calories   692
% Daily Value*
Total Fat 29.2g   37%
Saturated Fat 18.3g   91%
Cholesterol 76mg 25%
Sodium 224mg   10%
Total Carbohydrate 110g   40%
Dietary Fiber 1.3g 4%
Total Sugars 89.9g
Protein 5g

Chapter 7: Soups, Stews & Broths

Beef Stew

Preparation Time: 20 Minutes
Cooking Time: 50 Minutes
Yield: 6 Servings
Ingredients

4 tablespoons olive oil
2 pounds beef chuck cubed
½ teaspoon salt
½ teaspoon of freshly ground black pepper
1 onion, chopped
2 cloves garlic minced

3 tablespoons tomato paste
½ cup red wine
1 teaspoon dried rosemary
4 tablespoons Worcestershire sauce
2.5 cups beef stock
10 red potatoes, halved
3 carrots, peeled and chopped

Directions

Pre-heat the Oster Toaster oven to 300 degrees F.
Take a large cooking pot that fits inside the toaster oven.
Heat it over the flame and add olive oil. Then add beef and cook unit brown,
Season the beef with salt and black pepper.
Now add onion and cook for 5 more minutes
Then add all the remaining ingredients excluding beef stock and red wine.
Let the ingredients cook for 2 minutes. Then add broth and wine.
Cover the lid and put the pot in the Oster Toaster oven.
Bake it for 30 minutes. Then serve and enjoy.

Nutrition Facts
Servings: 6
Amount per serving
Calories   912
% Daily Value*
Total Fat 49g   63%
Saturated Fat 17.1g   85%
Cholesterol 157mg   52%
Sodium 779mg   34%
Total Carbohydrate 65.8g   24%
Dietary Fiber 7.7g 27%
Total Sugars 9g
Protein 48.9g

Hearty Beef Stew

Preparation Time: 20 Minutes
Cooking Time: 60 Minutes
Yield: 4 Servings
Ingredients
1 pound of Beef Stew Cubes
Salt and black pepper, to taste
2 Carrots, sliced
2 Can Cream of Mushroom Soup
4 tablespoons Dry Onion Soup Mix
2 Potatoes, cubed
10 ounces of Tomato Sauce
4 tablespoons of olive oil

Directions
Pre-heat the Oster Toaster oven to 350 degrees F.
Take a large cooking pot that fits inside the toaster oven.
Heat it over the flame and add olive oil.
Then add beef and cook unit brown.
Season the beef with salt and black pepper.
Now add potatoes and carrots and cook for 10 more minutes.
Then add all the remaining ingredients.
Let the ingredients cook for 5 minutes.
Cover the pot with the lid and put the pot in an Oster Toaster oven.
Bake it for 40 minutes. Then serve and enjoy.

Nutrition Facts
Servings: 4
Amount per serving
Calories   501
% Daily Value*
Total Fat 32.5g   42%
Saturated Fat 7.7g 39%
Cholesterol 26mg 9%
Sodium 1805mg   78%
Total Carbohydrate 42.7g   16%
Dietary Fiber 5.4g 19%
Total Sugars 7.9g
Protein 12.4g

Cream of Tomato Soup

Preparation Time: 20 Minutes
Cooking Time: 30 Minutes
Yield: 3 Servings
Ingredients
2 cups tomato juice
2 tablespoons of butter or margarine
1 1/2 teaspoon of brown sugar
Black pepper and Salt, pinch
¼ teaspoon of onion powder
¼ teaspoon of celery salt
1/4 cup potato juice
2 cups of coconut milk

Directions
Take a blender and pulse the tomatoes for a few minutes.
Then add butter, sugar, onion powder, pepper, celery salt, and potato juice in a blender and pulse
Then pour this into a cooking pot and add milk.
Transfer it to the Oster Toaster oven.
Turn on the Oster Toaster oven and set the temperate to 400 degrees F.
Put the pot inside the Oster Toaster oven and let it bake for 30 minutes.
Once it's warm, serve.

Nutrition Facts
Servings: 3
Amount per serving
Calories   470
% Daily Value*
Total Fat 45.8g   59%
Saturated Fat 35.1g   175%
Cholesterol 0mg   0%
Sodium 550mg   24%
Total Carbohydrate 17.5g   6%
Dietary Fiber 4.2g 15%
Total Sugars 12.7g
Protein

Chicken Soup

Preparation Time: 25 Minutes
Cooking Time: 60 Minutes
Yield: 2 Servings
Ingredients
1 teaspoon of lemon juice
1 /2 teaspoon of black pepper
2 cups shredded chicken
Salt, to taste
1 teaspoon of garlic, minced
1 cup carrots, chopped
1 cup celery, diced
4 cups chicken broth

Directions
Mix the shredded chicken with salt, black pepper, garlic, and lemon juice.
Take a baking pan and place cubed carrots, onions, and celery.
Put chicken pieces on top of the vegetables in a baking rack.
Pour two cups of chicken broth into the pan.
Cover the pan and put it in an Oster Toaster oven.
Bake it for1 an hour at 400 degrees F.

Nutrition Facts
Servings: 2
Amount per serving
Calories   246
% Daily Value*
Total Fat 4.4g   6%
Saturated Fat 1.2g 6%
Cholesterol 108mg   36%
Sodium 245mg   11%
Total Carbohydrate 7.8g 3%
Dietary Fiber 2.3g 8%
Total Sugars 3.4g
Protein 41.5g

Chicken, Potatoes, Leek Soup

Preparation Time: 25 Minutes
Cooking Time: 60 Minutes
Yield: 4 Servings
Ingredients
2 teaspoons of lemon juice
1 /2 teaspoon of white pepper
1 pound chicken legs
Salt, to taste
1 teaspoon of ginger garlic paste
1 cup potatoes, peeled and diced
1 cup leeks, diced
4 cups of chicken broth
Directions
Rub the chicken legs with salt, white pepper, garlic and ginger paste, and lemon juice. Take a baking pan and put leeks, potatoes in it
Put chicken pieces on top of the vegetables in a baking rack.
Pour two cups of chicken broth into the pan.
Cover the pan and put it in an Oster Toaster oven.
Bake it for1 an hour at 400 degrees F.
Remove the baking pan from the Oster Toaster oven and then shred chicken pieces, mix it with the ingredients. Discard the bones.
Cook it for 10 more minutes in an Oster Toaster oven. Then serve and enjoy.

Nutrition Facts
Servings: 4
Amount per serving
Calories   295
% Daily Value*
Total Fat 9.9g   13%
Saturated Fat 2.7g 14%
Cholesterol 101mg   34%
Sodium 907mg   39%
Total Carbohydrate 10.2g   4%
Dietary Fiber 1.4g 5%
Total Sugars 2.1g
Protein 38.7g

Chicken Stew

Preparation Time: 25 Minutes
Cooking Time: 50 Minutes
Yield: 4 Servings
Ingredients
2 boneless skinless chicken breasts, halved
1/3 teaspoon of lemon zest
1/3 cup olive oil
1 tablespoon Italian seasoning mix
Salt and pepper, to taste
1 small zucchini, sliced
5 ounces mushrooms, sliced
1 medium red pepper, sliced
1 leek, sliced
2 tablespoons white wine
1 cup of vegetable broth

Directions
Take a bowl and combine oil, lemon zest, herbs and salt, and black pepper.
Then put in the chicken breasts and mix well.
Take a baking pan and put chicken breast pieces in it.
Then add all the remaining ingredients
Fold packet the baking pan and place it in the Oster Toaster oven
 Bake at 400 degrees F, for 50 minutes.
Serve with brown rice.

Nutrition Facts
Servings: 4
Amount per serving
Calories   334
% Daily Value*
Total Fat 22.9g   29%
Saturated Fat 4g   20%
Cholesterol 65mg   22%
Sodium 264mg   11%
Total Carbohydrate 8g   3%
Dietary Fiber 1.5g 5%
Total Sugars 3.7g
Protein 24.4g

Shrimp Soup

Preparation Time: 25 Minutes
Cooking Time: 40 Minutes
Yield: 3 Servings
Ingredients
1 cup tomato paste
3 cups vegetable broth
1 cup mushrooms, sliced
1/4 cup, green bell pepper
2 cloves garlic, minced
1 teaspoon of lemon t zest, sliced
½ teaspoon of savory leaves
1.5 pounds shrimp, peeled, deveined
Salt and black pepper, to taste

Directions
Combine all ingredients in a shallow baking pan and cover it with foil.
Put it in an Oster Toaster oven and set the temperature to 400 degrees F.
Bake it for about 4o minutes.
Once it is ready, serve.

Nutrition Facts
Servings: 3
Amount per serving
Calories   388
% Daily Value*
Total Fat 5.7g   7%
Saturated Fat 1.6g 8%
Cholesterol 478mg   159%
Sodium 1404mg   61%
Total Carbohydrate 22.3g   8%
Dietary Fiber 3.9g 14%
Total Sugars 11.8g
Protein 61.1g

Chicken Corn Soup

Preparation Time: 25 Minutes
Cooking Time: 60 Minutes
Yield: 3 Servings
Ingredients
2 teaspoons of lemon juice
1 tablespoon of soy sauce
Salt and black pepper, to taste
2 cups chicken, boneless and shredded
1 teaspoon of garlic, minced
1 teaspoon of ginner minced
½ cup carrots, chopped
½ cup bell peppers, diced
1 can sweet corn, drained
2-3 cups of chicken broth

Directions
Mix the shredded chicken with salt, black pepper, garlic, ginger, soy sauce, and lemon juice.
Take a shallow baking pan and fit inside the Oster Toaster oven
Put the cubed carrots, bell peppers, and corn.
Put chicken pieces on top of the vegetables.
Pour chicken broth into the pan.
Cover the pan with a lid or use aluminum foil.
Place it in an Oster Toaster oven.
Bake it for 1 hour at 400 degrees F. Serve hot.

Nutrition Facts
Servings: 3
Amount per serving
Calories   255
% Daily Value*
Total Fat 5.3g   7%
Saturated Fat 1.4g 7%
Cholesterol 72mg 24%
Sodium 1399mg   61%
Total Carbohydrate 15g 5%
Dietary Fiber 2.2g 8%
Total Sugars 4.7g
Protein 36g

Cheesy Chicken & Broccoli Soup

Preparation Time: 25 Minutes
Cooking Time: 50 Minutes
Yield: 3 Servings
Ingredients
2 teaspoons coconut oil
1 yellow onion, diced
1 teaspoon of garlic, minced
1 teaspoon of cumin
1 cup of broccoli florets, fresh or frozen
1 pound of chicken pieces, boneless
2 cups of chicken broth
1 cup of coconut milk
Salt and black pepper, to taste
½ cup of cheddar cheese

Directions
Combine chicken with garlic, cumin, salt, and black pepper.
Add it to the baking pan and put onions, broccoli, and chicken broth.
Bake it in the Oster Toaster oven for 40 minutes at 400 degrees F, covered
Afterward, take out the baking pan and uncover it.
 Take out the chicken pieces.
Shred the chicken pieces and put them back in the Oster Toaster oven.
Also pour in the coconut milk and cheddar cheese.
Let it bake for 10 more minutes in an Oster Toaster oven. Then serve.

Nutrition Facts
Servings: 2
Amount per serving
Calories   936
% Daily Value*
Total Fat 61g   78%
Saturated Fat 40.3g   201%
Cholesterol 232mg   77%
Sodium 1216mg   53%
Total Carbohydrate 15.5g   6%
Dietary Fiber 5g   18%
Total Sugars 7.7g
Protein 81.7g

Butternut Squash Soup

Preparation Time: 25 Minutes
Cooking Time: 55 Minutes
Yield: 4-6 Servings
Ingredients

1 Butternut Squash peeled and cubed
2 large Onions, chopped
2 cloves Garlic chopped
1 teaspoon fresh ginger minced
2 teaspoons curry powder
 5 ounces can of coconut milk
6 cups vegetable stock
Salt and Pepper to taste

Directions

Take a baking pan and add butternut squash, onions, garlic, ginger, curry powder, salt, pepper, and vegetable stock.
Mix and then put it in an Oster Toaster oven.
Let it bake for45 minutes at 400 degrees F.
Take out eh baking pan and add coconut milk.
Transfer the ingredient to a blender and blend until smooth.
Pour the soup into the pan and let it bake for 10 more minutes.
Once done, serve and enjoy.

Nutrition Facts
Servings: 6
Amount per serving
Calories   119
% Daily Value*
Total Fat 6.5g   8%
Saturated Fat 5.3g 27%
Cholesterol 3mg   1%
Sodium 303mg   13%
Total Carbohydrate 13.4g   5%
Dietary Fiber 3.3g 12%
Total Sugars 7.6g
Protein 2.2g

Chapter 8: Beans And Eggs

Baked Beans

Preparation Time: 25 Minutes
Cooking Time: 30 Minutes
Yield: 4 Servings
Ingredients
2 cans of Pork & Beans, 7 ounces
½ white onion, diced
1 sausage, diced
1/2 pound bacon, diced
¼ cup ketchup
1 teaspoon white vinegar
3/4 cup brown sugar
Directions
Take a skillet and fry onions in it along with bacon and sausage.
Drain the excess fat.
Put the pork and sausage in a bowl and add vinegar, brown sugar, and ketchup.
Add the prepared bacon mix in it.
Put it in a casserole dish.
Bake it in the Oster Toaster oven for 30 minutes at 300 degrees F.
Once done, serve.

Nutrition Facts
Servings: 4
Amount per serving
Calories   635
% Daily Value*
Total Fat 31.3g   40%
Saturated Fat 9.8g 49%
Cholesterol 68mg 23%
Sodium 2581mg   112%
Total Carbohydrate 58.1g   21%
Dietary Fiber 9.2g 33%
Total Sugars 34.9g
Protein 30.9g

Toaster Oven Egg Bake

Preparation Time: 25 Minutes
Cooking Time: 25-30 Minutes
Yield: 2 Servings
Ingredients
4 large eggs
1/3 cup cottage cheese,
1/2 cup shredded pepper jack cheese, 2 ounces
1 jalapeño, chopped
1/3 cup corn, drained
Salt and black pepper, to taste
Oil spray, for greasing

Directions
Preheat the Oster Toaster oven to 350 degrees F, by turning on the bake function.
Grease a baking dish with oil spray.
Whisk eggs in a bowl and add cottage cheese, pepper jack cheese, corn, salt, pepper, and jalapeno.
Pour the egg into the baking dish.
Bake for 25 minutes until eggs firm.
Add more time if needed
Serve and enjoy.

Nutrition Facts
Servings: 2
Amount per serving
Calories   229
% Daily Value*
Total Fat 13.3g   17%
Saturated Fat 5.1g 26%
Cholesterol 383mg   128%
Sodium 339mg   15%
Total Carbohydrate 7.4g 3%
Dietary Fiber 0.9g 3%
Total Sugars 2g
Protein 20.4g

Egg On Cloud

Preparation Time: 25 Minutes
Cooking Time: 5-8 Minutes
Yield: 1 Serving
Ingredients
2 whole eggs, separated
2 teaspoons vegan margarine
2 sprouted bread, toasted
Pepper and salt, to taste

Directions
Preheat the Oster Toaster oven to broil function.
Toast the bread in an Oster Toaster oven.
Take two ramekins and a bowl.
Separate the egg whites in a bowl and egg yolk in ramekins
Whip the egg white until stiff peak stage from on top.
Put the margarine on the toasted oven and divide the egg white on top of the toast.
Make a hole in the middle of the egg whites on each piece of toast.
Put the egg yolk in middles
Sprinkle salt and pepper.
Place it under the broiler and let the egg cooked, but not burnt.
After 5 minutes take out and serve.

Nutrition Facts
Servings: 1
Amount per serving
Calories   373
% Daily Value*
Total Fat 18.3g   23%
Saturated Fat 4g   20%
Cholesterol 327mg   109%
Sodium 512mg   22%
Total Carbohydrate 30.8g   11%
Dietary Fiber 4g   14%
Total Sugars 4.7g
Protein 21.2g

Baked Italian Eggs

Preparation Time: 20 Minutes
Cooking Time: 12 Minutes
Yield: 4 Servings
Ingredients
4 organic eggs
1/3 cup marinara sauce
1/3 cup parmesan cheese, grated
1/3 cup mozzarella cheese, shredded
2 tablespoons cream, heavy
Salt and black pepper to taste
 Oil spray, for greasing

Directions
Preheat the Oster Toaster oven to400 degrees F.
Grease ramekins with oil spray and crack 2 eggs in one ramekin.
Then add cream and top it with cheese
Cook for 12 minutes at 325 degrees F in the Oster Toaster oven
Remove it from the oven and sprinkle salt and black pepper on top.
Put marinara sauce on top and serve.
Enjoy.

Nutrition Facts
Servings: 4
Amount per serving
Calories   192
% Daily Value*
Total Fat 12.9g   16%
Saturated Fat 6.1g 31%
Cholesterol 186mg   62%
Sodium 423mg   18%
Total Carbohydrate 4.5g 2%
Dietary Fiber 0.6g 2%
Total Sugars 2.3g
Protein 15.6g

Oster Toaster Oven Eggs

Preparation Time: 25 Minutes
Cooking Time: 15 Minutes
Yield: 4 Servings
Ingredients
4 large eggs
1/2 cup Tomato Sauce
2 tablespoons heavy cream
3 tablespoons of parmesan
2 tablespoons grated Fontina Cheese
Salt & Pepper to Taste
Oil spray, for greasing

Directions
Set the Oster Toaster oven to preheat at 420 degrees F.
Grease 4 ramekins with oil spray and add ¼ cup of tomato sauce, 1 whole egg, and top it with an equal amount of cream and grated cheeses.
Put it in the oven and let it bake until bubbly from the top.
Serve and enjoy with a sprinkle of salt and black pepper.

Nutrition Facts
Servings: 4
Amount per serving
Calories   122
% Daily Value*
Total Fat 9.1g   12%
Saturated Fat 4.1g 21%
Cholesterol 201mg   67%
Sodium 271mg   12%
Total Carbohydrate 2.4g 1%
Dietary Fiber 0.5g   2%
Total Sugars 1.8g
Protein 8.1g

Baked French Toast

Preparation Time: 20 Minutes
Cooking Time: 15 Minutes
Yield: 1 Serving
Ingredients
1 large organic egg
1 teaspoon vanilla extract
1 tablespoon brown sugar
1/4 teaspoon cinnamon
dash of sea salt
1 tablespoon butter, melted
1/2 cup almond milk
4 slices Texas toast, toasted

Directions
Preheat the Oster Toaster oven to 400 degrees F.
Take a bowl and mix egg, vanilla, brown sugar, cinnamon, and sea salt.
Then add melted butter.
Then pour in the almond milk.
Pour this mixture into a shallow bowl.
Soak the bread slice in the mixture and arrange it on a baking sheet.
Bake it at 425 degrees F for10 minutes.
Switch the function to broil and then broil it for 5 minutes. Sere and enjoy.

Nutrition Facts
Servings: 1
Amount per serving
Calories   897
% Daily Value*
Total Fat 49.1g   63%
Saturated Fat 34.2g   171%
Cholesterol 217mg   72%
Sodium 1247mg   54%
Total Carbohydrate 92.9g   34%
Dietary Fiber 6.9g 25%
Total Sugars 21.7g
Protein 21.2g

Hardboiled Egg

Preparation Time: 20 Minutes
Cooking Time: 35-40 Minutes
Yield: 2 Servings
Ingredients
4 eggs
1 teaspoon of vinegar
Pinch of salt
4-6 cups of water

Directions
Preheat the Oster Toaster oven to 325 degrees F.
Then take a shallow baking dish and fill the dish with the water-vinegar and salt.
Put it in the oven.
Once water simmers, put eggs in the baking dish.
Let it bake for 30 minutes.
Put it in ice water.
Peel and serve.

Nutrition Facts
Servings: 2
Amount per serving
Calories   126
% Daily Value*
Total Fat 8.8g   11%
Saturated Fat 2.7g 14%
Cholesterol 327mg   109%
Sodium 215mg   9%
Total Carbohydrate 0.7g 0%
Dietary Fiber 0g   0%
Total Sugars 0.7g
Protein 11.1g

Sunny-Side up Eggs

Preparation Time: 20 Minutes
Cooking Time: 12-15 Minutes
Yield: 2 Servings
Ingredients
2 eggs, organic
Cooking spray, for greasing
Salt and black pepper, to taste

Directions
Take a loaf pan and grease it with oil spray.
Crack the egg in the pan and then place it in the toaster oven.
Toast it until personal preference is achieved.
Sprinkle salt and pepper to taste.

Nutrition Facts
Servings: 2
Amount per serving
Calories   66
% Daily Value*
Total Fat 4.7g   6%
Saturated Fat 1.4g 7%
Cholesterol 164mg   55%
Sodium 62mg   3%
Total Carbohydrate 0.4g 0%
Dietary Fiber 0g   0%
Total Sugars 0.3g
Protein 5.6g

Egg Omelet

Preparation Time: 20 Minutes
Cooking Time: 20 Minutes
Yield: 2 Serving
Ingredients
4 organic eggs
1/4 cup almond milk
1/2 cup cheese, shredded
1 teaspoon of olive oil
¼ cup cooked mushrooms
4 pepperoncini chilies, sliced
1/2 tablespoon green onions, sliced
Salt and black pepper, to taste

Directions
Preheat the Oster Toaster oven to 350 degrees F.
Use a skillet to cook mushroom in oil for a few minutes.
Then put it on a dish
Break the egg into cups and then put it in a large bowl.
Put in with mushroom and mix all the listed ingredients as well.
Transfer it to a small baking pan.
Bake it for 20 minutes
Once the omelet is set, serve, and enjoy.

Nutrition Facts
Servings: 2
Amount per serving
Calories   331
% Daily Value*
Total Fat 27.6g   35%
Saturated Fat 15.4g   77%
Cholesterol 357mg   119%
Sodium 304mg   13%
Total Carbohydrate 3.1g 1%
Dietary Fiber 0.8g   3%
Total Sugars 2g
Protein 19.1g

Cheese Omelet

Preparation Time: 20 Minutes
Cooking Time: 35 Minutes
Yield: 4 Serving
Ingredients
8 bacon strips, diced
4 green onions, sliced
8 large eggs
1 cup milk
1/2 teaspoon seasoned salt
2-1/2 cups Monterey Jack cheese, divided

Directions
Preheat the Oster Toaster oven to 350 degrees F.
Take a skillet and cook bacon in it until crisp.
Set the bacon aside.
Sauté the onions, until tender in the bacon drippings.
Set it aside for further use.
Take a bowl and beat eggs in it
Then add milk, bacon, and seasoned salt along with sautéed onion and cheese.
Transfer it to a greased shallow dish.
Bake uncovered for 30-35 minutes. Once done, serve and enjoy.

Nutrition Facts
Servings: 4
Amount per serving
Calories   509
% Daily Value*
Total Fat 37.3g   48%
Saturated Fat 15.6g   78%
Cholesterol 427mg   142%
Sodium 1104mg   48%
Total Carbohydrate 9.3g 3%
Dietary Fiber 2.4g 9%
Total Sugars 4.2g
Protein 32.7g

Conclusion

No doubt the Oster Toaster oven is one of the solid appliances that is a unique addition to your kitchen to keep meals fresh. The feedback and the sales of this appliance make it top convection ovens that fulfill all your cooking needs and wants. It also comes in handy for those with less space and a smaller kitchen. Now preparing mouthwatering and delicious count top oven recipes is not a problem. This cookbook provides you with all the information necessary to buy an Oster Toaster oven and also start making recipes as a beginner.

We hope you like our efforts.

Printed in the USA
CPSIA information can be obtained
at www.ICGtesting.com
LVHW052038300923
759761LV00007B/184